Lampedusa pie

Lampedusa pie

Andrea Burgener

photography by Theana Breugem

CONTENTS

PLAY WITH YOUR FOOD   143

STRETCH & EXPLORE   163

LAMPEDUSA PIE

INTRODUCTION

A few weeks before our third baby was due (I knew at that stage that I'd need a Caesarean section), I had a dream in which I was being wheeled into an operating theatre, nurse at my side. 'What are you in for?' asked the nurse. 'A Caesar,' I replied. Her response surprised me, even in my dream: 'So will that be the classic Caesar or the chicken Caesar?'

Clearly, I am obsessed with food. And that, I suppose, is my chief food credential. I think about things I could cook just about every minute of my waking time.

I had no formal training when I opened my first restaurant, just years of non-stop cooking, and my approach is still probably more like that of a home cook than a professional chef, even if I do cook for a living. The recipes in this book are all over the road in terms of style, history, everything. They are partly, I guess, the result of my upbringing in the fractured, shifting city of Johannesburg, where I have lived all my life. And I am, as are most current cooks, constantly bombarded with a thousand recipes, sources and food images. I am a magpie cook. I am fickle and disloyal to many dishes. But not to all: the dishes that spring from nostalgia I am foolishly attached to. If you're the nostalgic sort, Johannesburg is an especially weird city in which to grow up. You are forever watching your favourite places disappear. There is of course no innocence in nostalgia, in a country with a history such as ours (indeed, many argue that nostalgia is always a very dodgy and reactionary state). I recognise that, but can't pretend that my own childhood was anything but happy.

Many of these recipes are ones we cooked in the various restaurants I've had at one or other time – Superbonbon, Deluxe I and Deluxe II, and The Leopard. Others are old family recipes, and some went in because on that day, they were what I wanted to cook.

Why is this book called *Lampedusa Pie*? Flip to the recipe on page 192 for the lowdown. It's a dish that is all about nostalgia. If you think the title is a bit odd, consider others that came close (suggested by my children): *I Love Big Food, The Book of Mad Food, The Remote of Fire*, and *The Gods' No. 1 Cookbook*.

So that I don't have to repeatedly mention free-range eggs, grass-fed beef, sustainably-sourced seafood (though, as you will see, I have not been able to restrain myself here and there), let me say it here: wherever I say eggs, please take them to mean free range. Because not all free range is so very free, I'd urge you to do some poking about. Wherever I say beef, I mean pasture-reared rather than feedlot (cows aren't actually supposed to eat grain, a huge surprise to modern urban diners); and when I say chicken I mean non-battery, which is basically any chicken that doesn't have something contrary to this printed somewhere on the packaging, no matter how swanky the supermarket in which you found it. The best advice I can give any eater is to go out and buy Michael Pollan's *Omnivore's Dilemma*. Not a cookbook, but the best book about food you will ever read.

Good luck.

BREAKFAST & BEYOND

The greatest breakfast on earth, and this is actually fact, is yum cha – that incredible Cantonese free-form tea-time banquet made up of dozens of dim sum. I haven't given the recipes for any of these because what you do is eat them at a dim sum restaurant, with steaming bamboo baskets of puffy dumplings and slippery rice rolls all about you, and much noise, green tea and whisky completing the picture. You don't make them at home unless you're crazy, a hermit, or both. Okay, I had to talk about yum cha – obsessed, can't help myself. Second to yum cha, I like to think, are the recipes that follow here. The 'beyond' part is to emphasise that these dishes are just as right for dinner, lunch or a midnight snack as they are for breakfast. Of course, you already know that pumpkin fritters and eggs Benedict are perfect for Sunday supper, you don't need me to tell you – I'm just giving you an extra nudge in that direction.

PUMPKIN **FRITTERS**

Is there a soul alive who can't be swayed by a good pumpkin fritter? These are lovely little things; just make them and see for yourself. Usually viewed as a pudding or tea-time snack of sorts, they are an even more glorious breakfast. They should be copiously doused with cinnamon sugar and, with each new bite, dunked into cream.

Mix together the pumpkin, flour, sugar, cinnamon, salt and egg, and mix to make a soft, droppable batter.

If it seems too firm, even tough (the particular pumpkin or butternut will determine this), add another egg to the mix, and if need be some extra flour to compensate. These fritters are relaxed and unskittish things, and can take some tweaking.

In a good, thick-bottomed pan, heat the oil. Drop a tiny bit of batter in. If it bubbles gently, the oil is ready. Drop about two dessertspoons in for each fritter, and fry gently until brown on the underside, then flip and ditto the second side.

Test one. If the batter is still slightly damp/raw in the middle, place the fritters in the oven for about 10 minutes to cook through.

While still very hot, dust the fritters with the sugar-cinnamon mix and serve post-haste with cream on the side. If eating for breakfast, poached spiced apples or a similar concoction go eagerly with these fritters.

SERVES FOUR

500 g pumpkin or butternut, steamed or boiled, and mashed smoothish (some little lumps are fine)

1 cup self-raising flour

30 ml light brown sugar

¾ teaspoon ground cinnamon

½ teaspoon salt

1 egg

Vegetable oil for shallow frying

¼ cup sugar and cinnamon (equal parts) for dusting

PISTACHIO-ROLLED LABNEH WITH POACHED PEARS

Labneh is one of those easy cheeses for cheats – you feel very clever to have created it, but, like making paneer (see page 146), it's child's play and requires no special equipment. You're basically just draining the liquid from yoghurt, leaving behind a creamier, more solid mass. It's ridiculously delicious. Try it once, and you'll make it again at the drop of a hat. Unlike savoury labneh, you can't store this in olive oil, so its shelf life is short – about the same length as the yoghurt it came from.

Line the colander or sieve with the kitchen cloth, and set it over the bowl. Mix the yoghurt and syrup together, pour it into the cloth and close the cloth over the mass loosely. Leave in the fridge for two days, or until enough whey has drained off for the yoghurt to be firm enough to shape. Sometimes this takes only 24 hours, sometimes up to three days.

Remove from the fridge, and roll into litchi-sized balls. Put the pistachios on a plate, then roll the labneh balls through the nuts to coat more or less evenly. This part can be done up to a few hours before serving.

When ready to eat, divide the little jade balls between two shallow bowls and add a few spoons of syrupy fruit (the labneh likes quite a bit of liquid). Squeeze lemon juice over everything and grate the lemon zest over nano-seconds before serving.

FOR TWO PORTIONS (MAKES ABOUT ONE CUP)

2 cups full-cream real yoghurt (sometimes 'pretend' yoghurts made with cornstarch or other binding agents won't separate into liquid and solid, so use real yoghurt made with just milk and cultures)

1 tablespoon maple syrup (use plain golden syrup if you don't have real maple: the taste of fake maple is overbearing)

1 very clean kitchen cloth (loose weave el cheapo style) and one sieve or colander over a deep bowl

To serve

½ cupful chopped pistachio nuts (hazelnuts are also very good, but pistachios win on looks)

Good bottled fruit, in syrup (I like to use pears poached in a star anise-spiked syrup, but apples and prunes also work well. You could also serve the labneh with fresh chopped fruit that has been macerated in sweetened orange juice.)

Juice of ½ lemon (essential, I think, as the syrup can otherwise be cloying)

Zest of ½ lemon

LAMPEDUSA PIE

FRENCH TOAST THE RIGHT WAY

A recipe for French toast might seem unnecessary. Well, I don't think so, because most home-made and restaurant French toast I get is plain horrible. Though there isn't much to it, what there is has to be done right.

Firstly – and though this might seem painfully obvious, it's the biggest error made – you must start with good bread. Stale or fresh, it doesn't matter, but it must be proper bread, by which I mean bread that has proved over time rather than suffering the speed-proving that 99 per cent of all supermarket bread endures, with gluten, yeast, improvers and other rubbish added to compensate for the cheating. I would never deny the marshmallowy charms this sort of bread holds when used for a late-night peanut butter and syrup sandwich or a braaibroodjie (even if I'm opposed to it in theory), but the problem is using it in cooking, or where it needs to make contact with much liquid. Immediately, the added gluten forms a mucousy gloopiness, and the lack of real structure is exposed as the bread buckles and compacts within the liquid. You are left with wet cotton wool. What this means, then, is getting your bread from a proper baker, or doing some intensive label checking.

The second error comes with the soaking. A quick flip in the egg mix is not good enough: you need to soak the bread well (which is precisely why you need good bread). There is no point at all to French toast that is dry in the middle – the contrast between the browned outside and the soufflé-ish soft eggy middle is what it's all about.

Heat the oil until some egg mix dropped in sizzles languidly. Slide floppy bread slices in carefully, pour the remaining egg mix over and around them, and fry on both sides until browned and the egg is cooked through to the centre. Eat all fraying egg-mix bits that seem to be extra as you go. Keep warm in a low oven if you have any more to make.

Serve absolutely immediately. I'm sure you know what you want as an accompaniment, but let me just mention that a bowl of hot berry compote plus cream, or loads of crack-crisp bacon, and a squeeze of fresh lemon and syrup are almost unbeatable. Or pair it with the tomato-chilli-ginger relish on page 99, as I do in the restaurant. Marmite, though, might be best of all.

FOR EACH PERSON

2 slices thickly cut ciabatta, sourdough or kitka (panettone makes a mean sweet French toast too)

2 eggs beaten with 4 tablespoons cream, dash of cinnamon and good pinch of salt

About 2 tablespoons best vegetable oil for cooking (grapeseed oil is good)

LEEKY **BREAD-AND-BUTTER PUDDING**

My clever friend Louise, a hugely talented 'natural' cook, who worked the hob with us like a demon for 18 months in the kitchen of my former restaurant, Deluxe, and still guest 'hobs' at The Leopard, adapted this recipe – for the better, I'm sure – from some obscure source. Having worked by instinct, she could only give me estimates on the thing, so this is my adaption of her adaption. It's laughably simple, but does need some careful bread buying: a good-quality kitka, Portuguese loaf or soft ciabatta all work well. Don't even think of using a cotton-woolly supermarket loaf (see the recipe for French toast, on page 15, for why you shouldn't). You can adapt this in all sorts of ways, the only proviso being to stick to the same egg:cream:milk ratio.

Leave the leeks to soak in cold water, to make sure all the fine soil works its way out of them. Preheat the oven to 180 °C.

Heat the olive oil and butter in a heavy-bottomed pan and sauté the leeks on a low heat until soft and even starting to get a caramelised tone. Season and take off the heat.

Mix the eggs, cream, nutmeg, Parmesan and salt in a large, shallow bowl.

Butter an oven dish of more or less 20 cm diameter. It shouldn't be too deep, or smaller than this diameter, or the ratio of custardy inside to crusty topping will be wrong. Line the base with half the bread, spread the leeks on top, then top with the remaining bread, overlapping like fish scales (this is not done for looks, but so that you have more crusty edges).

Pour the egg mix over the bread and leave to soak for about 15 minutes. Place the dish in the centre of the oven and bake for around 30 minutes or until obviously set, and golden-brown on the top.

Eat immediately. It's good as is, but I especially like it with baked tomatoes on the side. Also, as you've no doubt guessed, it's ridiculously delicious with blue cheese in place of the Parmesan (or why not as well as the Parmesan?).

If eating it for lunch rather than breakfast, brunch or a midnight snack, a big pile of vinaigrette-tossed leaves is the perfect addition.

FOR TWO QUITE HUNGRY PEOPLE

2 cups leeks (when raw), sliced chunkily

2 tablespoons olive oil plus 1 tablespoon butter

4 eggs

2 cups single cream

Sprinkle of nutmeg

2 tablespoons grated Parmesan

4 slices good ciabatta, Portuguese loaf or kitka bread, cut into big pieces

Good salt for leeks and custard (about ¾ teaspoon for each)

CILBIR (POACHED EGGS WITH GARLIC YOGHURT AND PAPRIKA SAGE BUTTER)

Usually (or so I read) served as a hot meze dish or snack in Turkey, this makes one of the most delicious breakfasts you could ever hope to fall upon. It begs to be eaten with hot fresh pita bread or, failing that, good sourdough bread, torn rather than sliced.

If you have egg-poaching neurosis, which I have discovered many do, just make the dish with soft-boiled eggs. It works just as well (only doesn't look quite as elegant).

Stir the garlic into the yoghurt. Spread over two plates to form little beds for the eggs.

Boil a small pot of water, add the vinegar and gently lower first the egg into the water. Feel free to do the whirlpool thing if you like, but it never seems to make a difference to my poaching endeavours. The critical thing is that the eggs are very fresh, or the whites will just rag and feather through the water.

Keep the water on a low boil and cook each egg for about three minutes (for soft-yolk eggs), keeping others warm under a lid on a warm plate.

While the eggs are cooking, melt the butter in a pan, stir in the sage leaves (if fresh, make sure they fry till crispy) or parsley, add the paprika and take off the heat while you deal with the eggs.

Remove the eggs with a slotted spoon and place on the yoghurt.

Spoon the paprika butter over the eggs, season and eat with great haste (which means remembering to heat the pita bread just before the eggs are ready).

SERVES TWO

2 garlic cloves, very finely slivered

2½ cups thick, creamy plain yoghurt

2 to 3 teaspoons white wine vinegar, for poaching eggs

4 very fresh eggs, cracked into small container

2 tablespoons butter

A few fresh or dried sage leaves (crumbled if dried) or flat-leaf parsley

1 teaspoon best paprika

Best salt and freshly ground pepper

Pita bread

APPLE & ONION **ATCHAR**

I call it atchar, but it's not much like the bottled atchars you buy, because there is much less oil, so don't be scared off (or dismayed, if the oil is what you like about commercial atchar). Unlike the long-life oily fellows, it will last only about two weeks in the fridge. It's multivalent, extremely delicious and very quick to knock together. I love this piled onto Brie and warmed in the oven, just until the Brie starts to melt. Also brilliant with braaied meats, Cheddar cheese, and with 'mighty pata' (see the recipe on page 166).

Heat the oil and sauté the onions on a low heat until translucent and softening. Add the apples and chilli, and keep frying on a lowish heat.

When the apple is soft, turn up the heat to caramelise a little. Add turmeric, stir through, then add the vinegar, sugar and salt, check balance and adjust. Bear in mind that when you're eating it cool, the intensity of the chilli, sugar and vinegar will be lessened.

Leave to cool.

MAKES ONE BOTTLE

3 tablespoons sunflower or grapeseed oil

2 onions, peeled and cut into slightly smaller pieces than the apple

3 Granny Smith apples, peeled and cut into blocks

1 Thai chilli, finely chopped, seeds removed if you want it mild

½ teaspoon turmeric

3 tablespoons rice vinegar or white grape vinegar

Sugar to taste – about 1 dessertspoon

Salt to taste (more than you expect)

ATHOL BROSE IN A BOWL

The 'bowl' part is there to differentiate this glorious porridge dish from the original Scottish Athol Brose breakfast, which is served as a drink of sorts. The original recipe calls for the oats to be soaked in whisky and whisky alone. This is a bit hardcore for those of us who haven't been up since 5 am roaming the Highlands, so I've adapted it slightly. It's still a pretty stiff breakfast, but as most of the alcohol is cooked off, it's not as lethal as it sounds. Amounts are vague because everyone has their own idea of the perfect consistency, saltiness, etc., for porridge. I think a quite thick, fairly salty, very buttery and not too sweet mix is right, with an added dash of whisky at the end, plus cinnamon.

Soak the oats (follow instructions on the box for the per-person amounts) in a half-half mix of whisky and milk, with enough liquid to completely cover the oats. Soak for anything from an hour to overnight.

To cook: pour the oat mix into a thick-bottomed pan, place on a low heat and add cold milk, stirring all the while, until you have a thick, creamy consistency. Simmer on a low heat, covered, for another few minutes.

Add honey and salt to taste, plus a big knob of butter per serving. Add more whisky if you want an extra kick, and take off the heat. Serve immediately in warm bowls, with a sprinkle of cinnamon, and lots of cream and honey on the side.

Finish the bowl and have a lie-down.

EGGS BENEDICT
INCLUDING NO-SAFETY-BELT HOLLANDAISE

Popular wisdom has it that you go to hell in a hand-basket, or at the very least end up with a miserable curdled mess, if you even think about making hollandaise without a double-boiler. But guess what? It's not actually strictly true. I promise. Hollandaise à la naked flame works just fine, and is a whole lot quicker.

Long ago, on a busy breakfast shift in my restaurant, when Mr Hollandaise Duty confessed too late that he hadn't made the sauce, we threw the nearest pot onto the hob, and went ahead with a straight-on-the-flame version. I always use this method now. Strictly, you're making something slightly removed from a true hollandaise, because some extra liquid is used to emulsify everything with less risk.

If you're still scared of getting a little brutal with hollandaise, consider the fact that until perhaps the early eighties, SAA used to serve eggs Benedict practically as their default breakfast on morning flights (true!) – and a good one it was too. Just a tad thick perhaps, but surely, if that hollandaise could survive the many-thousand-feet-high superfast reheat, and several hours standing around, it's not the quivering wallflower we are asked to respect in extremis.

To facilitate the naked-flame method, we start with the orange juice and beat the yolks into this first. The extra liquid means that you are now free to enact the apparently unthinkable direct-heat method, which, if you are very clever, also works on an electric hob. The trick is to be very bold about everything.

Mix yolks and orange juice in the pan, put onto a medium-low flame and add the blocks of cold butter bit by bit, whisking *all* the time. When forgetting to take our butter from the freezer before making this, we discovered that, if anything, it's easier, as the cold butter stabilises the sauce, which is always on the verge of becoming a little too hot. Keep whisking and adding the butter, and continue to mix until the sauce is pouring custard-thick. If it looks like curdling, whip it off the heat and add the ¼ cup of cold cream you've cunningly kept on standby. Lastly, add salt to taste.

Serve over warm English muffins, some good ham and a single soft-poached egg. I think two eggs is excessive, given the amount of egg in the sauce, but don't let me stop you.

3 to 4 egg yolks (depending on size), well beaten

2 to 3 tablespoons fresh orange juice

130 g best butter, cubed

Salt to taste

HOLLANDAISE FOR TWO TO THREE PORTIONS

Eggs Benedict deviations

Eggs Florentine – A few tablespoons of lightly steamed, seasoned, chopped spinach in place of ham. Creamed spinach is overkill under the hollandaise.

Eggs Loch Ness – Use a potato cake or mash instead of a muffin. This may seem odd, but the smooth texture of the potato is very flattering to the sauce, possibly more so than the crumble of a muffin.

Porcini mushrooms – My favourite combination of all these things is miles away from an original Benedict: try sautéed porcinis and mash topped with hollandaise, and skip the poached egg. Grind plenty of black pepper over it all. (For how to cook porcinis, refer to page 178).

LAMPEDUSA PIE

PROPER **ENGLISH MUFFINS**

Even good home-made eggs Benedict are usually only actually home-made from the waist up, as it were. But home-made English muffins are totally glorious. They're so easy to throw together that when you've made them once, you're unlikely to go back to the industrial version. And they're not just useful for taking eggs Benedict or Florentine to new heights. They're fantastic with pretty much anything for which you'd usually call upon toast or scones, my two favourite toppings being lots of butter and good honey, or lots of butter and a smudge of Marmite. My daughter Holly recently introduced me to butter sprinkled with plenty of sugar, which is very fine too.

The only thing that makes these muffins any more trouble than the simplest pancake is remembering to make the batter ahead. And, okay, there is some procuring to do (but please don't let this be a deterrent): a proper muffin ring or two, available from most baking shops or from professional catering suppliers, is indispensable. A muffin ring keeps the batter 'up' while it's still in its runny first moments, so that the end muffin is a thick, puffy disc, rather than a blini-ish thing.

Mix all the ingredients together in a large bowl or jug, making sure the vessel is only half full. Cover and leave to prove in the fridge, for anything from three hours to overnight.

To cook, ladle or pour the mix into greased muffin rings set on a lightly oiled flat-top grill or large pan. The batter should be about one finger thick.

Cook on a medium-low heat until bubbles on top are plentiful and the muffin is golden-brown underneath. I won't pretend that checking the muffin's underside isn't slightly annoying with the muffin ring in place, but there's nought one can do about that. Remove muffin ring, flip and cook the second side until golden-brown. The heat must *not* be high, or the muffins will be browned before the centres are cooked.

Keep warm in a low oven, covered with a kitchen cloth, while you proceed with the remaining batter.

English muffins can be reheated in a toaster or moderate oven, up to about three days later. This is second prize though – there's nothing quite like them fresh, straight off the stove, yielding, almost Chelsea-bunnish inside and crisp on the outside. Shop muffins just can't compete.

SERVES FOUR TO SIX

200 g white wheat flour (or white and brown flour mixed)

1 teaspoon yeast

1 free-range egg

1½ cups full-cream milk

Generous pinch of salt

APPLE & AUBERGINE **TARTE TATIN**

I know this sounds like some wacky, tacky combination for the sake of being different, but it's not: the combination of aubergine (brinjal) and apple is traditional in French Catalonia, on the Spanish border, and for good reason. Apple and aubergine are so very good to one another. This is made even better by being served with thick cream or, best of all, a slice of perfect Brie.

Preheat the oven to 190 °C.

Peel and core the apples, and slice them quite thinly. Peel and slice the aubergine even more thinly.

Melt the butter in the pan, then add the sugar and mix in a little. Let it caramelise on a medium heat, watching carefully. When it's golden-brown, remove the pan from the heat, pour the caramelly butter into a jug or bowl, arrange the slices of aubergine and apple in the pan, and pour the butter mix back on top.

Place in the oven for around 15 minutes. Remove, and spoon any syrupy juice from the pan base over the apple-aubergine layer. Place the pastry carefully on top, tucking into the edges.

Brush the pastry with the yolk (or milk) and bake for 30 minutes or until golden-brown.

Place a plate over the pan and flip over so that the pastry forms the base. Don't worry, even if some pieces stick to the pan, you just prise them off and re-lay them casually on top. Eat immediately.

FOR ONE TART, TO SERVE FOUR

Three green apples (Golden Delicious or Granny Smith)

1 large or 2 small aubergines

100 g butter

100 g sugar

Enough puff pastry (home-made or bought) to cover a 20 cm pan

1 egg yolk (or milk)

20 cm ovenproof pan

MARMALADE & APPLE **PUDDING CAKE**

I do sometimes feel it is slightly sacrilegious to change a Nigella Lawson recipe. What could the woman ever possibly do wrong in the kitchen? But, well, wondrous as the cake is, upon my first try with it I felt in my marrow that it would be yet more wondrous if it was even damper and slightly less sweet. And so I have grated in an apple and taken the sugar down from 150 g to 120 g. Eat this as a tea-time thing with whipped cream or as a pudding, with pouring cream.

Preheat oven to 180 °C.

Butter an ovenproof dish, about 24 cm square (or equivalent volume round).

Mix butter with sugar, marmalade and grated apple. Add eggs, flour and orange juice and zest.

Pour into cake dish, level the top and bake for around 30 minutes. A bit undercooked is preferable to over. While cooking, melt the remaining orange juice and the 80 g of marmalade together for the glaze.

Once the cake is out, dribble the marmalade topping all over. Eat immediately (best) or when cool (still excellent). If eating the next day, pour a bit of milk over it and reheat in the oven so it becomes even more puddingy.

MAKES ABOUT EIGHT TO TEN PORTIONS

250 g butter – softened at room temperature if summer, softened but not melted in a low oven if winter

120 g light brown sugar

160 g good marmalade (plus 80 g for glaze)

1 big Granny Smith or other green apple, grated

4 eggs

225 g self-raising flour

Juice of ½ orange (remaining juice reserved for glaze)

Zest of 1 orange

SHAKSHUKA

Bless you, Jonathan Dorfman, great friend and excellent cook, for putting me onto such a wondrous delight. This Middle Eastern stewy egg dish is the sort of thing you find yourself craving in the middle of the night, or upon waking with a small hangover. It's also an excellent Sunday-evening-supper solution.

The recipe is Claudia Roden's, with a minor tweak in the spicing, inspired by London chef Anna Hansen's The Modern Pantry Cookbook.

In a large skillet over medium heat, fry the spices in the oil for a minute or so, followed by the peppers until they soften. Add the garlic, and when it begins to colour just slightly, add the tomatoes, salt, pepper and harissa. Cook until the tomatoes soften.

Add the seasoning, then slide the eggs into the dish/pan in which the sauce is cooking. Crack them into a bowl first, and not directly into the stew: fishing micro-pieces of shell out of an opaque stewy mass is far more annoying than grabbing a bowl off a shelf.

Cook until the eggs are done to your liking (with the lid on if you want to ensure the whites get cooked on top). Serve hot with a great volume of soft white bread. Optionally, top it with chopped coriander leaf.

SERVES TWO

3 tablespoons vegetable or extra-virgin olive oil

½ teaspoon each ground cumin and fennel seeds

2 red and/or green peppers, cut into ribbons (I prefer red and I only like them roasted and skinned, but that's optional, time-consuming and not traditional. Up to you.)

3 to 4 cloves garlic, sliced

4 medium tomatoes, peeled and cut into about 8 pieces

Salt and pepper to taste

Harissa to taste (add gradually) – *see recipe below*

4 eggs

HARISSA

Soak chillies in water for 30 minutes until soft.

Drain and pound with garlic, spices and a little salt with a pestle and mortar, or blend in a food processor, adding just enough oil to make a soft paste.

Spoon into a jar. Keeps very well in the fridge.

SERVES TWO

60 g dried red chillies (stems and seeds removed)

4 cloves garlic

1 teaspoon ground caraway

1 teaspoon ground coriander

½ teaspoon salt

Extra-virgin olive oil

YET ANOTHER **CRÈME BRÛLÉE** RECIPE

Why? Because so many of them are travesties of what they should be. I grew up with the best of crème brûlées, so I feel strongly about the matter. My mother is a curious sort of cook: everyday items – even sandwiches – do not work out well at all. But strangely, when it comes to the dishes (mainly seventies classics) that are daunting to most home-cooks, she unfailingly triumphs. And I mean spookily so. As children we would wade through prison-grade school lunchboxes, and then come home to dine on perfect soufflés – cheese, baby-marrow, sorrel or lemon (not one, in decades, ever flopped), asparagus with flawless hollandaise or Béarnaise, perfect soft-centred glossy pavlovas, and impeccable crème caramel and crème brûlée .

Once we were taken on holiday to a hotel where, every morning, the French Creole kitchen team served a buffet including crème brûlée and crème caramel for breakfast. We were so impressed by this decadence. But when you think about it, why not? They're egg dishes, after all. Or something like French toast without the bread, and the caramel replacing the syrup.

Here are the rules: firstly, never follow the silly new fashion of pouring pre-melted caramel onto the custard base, creating a palate-shredding tectonic plate. The only way is to caramelise a thin layer of sugar sprinkled onto the custard, to form a paper-thin crust. The difference is massive. Secondly, the custard must be all cream, none of this half-milk business (crème brûlée is not upside-down crème caramel). Thirdly, the container must be shallow: it's critical to have a good, generous ratio of topping to custard. I part with the purists who insist on using a double-boiler for cooking the custard. It's just as smooth made in the oven if the temperature is correctly low.

Heat the oven to 130 °C.

Beat the yolks, sugar and vanilla together. Add the cream and mix in well.

Pour the custard mix through a fine sieve into another bowl or wide-mouthed jug. Never think of leaving out this step.

Boil the kettle. Place the ramekins into a roasting dish, put in the oven and pour the recently boiled water around the containers to halfway up the sides. Again, never be tempted to leave out this step. The custards will overheat, and heat through unevenly, without the water around them.

Bake for about 40 minutes or until the custards are set but still have a jelly wobble to them.

Cool completely – in the fridge if time is pressing.

To brûlée, scatter a thin, even layer of castor sugar over the surface, then using a blowtorch, a brûlée iron or the oven grill, brûlée until dark brown. If using the grill, make sure the custard is well chilled first, or else by the time the top is browned, the custard will have started to cook again.

Let the surface drop to room temperature before serving – the crust won't be hard if it's still warm.

SERVES FOUR TO SIX

4 yolks

3 to 4 dessertspoons castor sugar, depending on your tooth

Vanilla seeds scraped from the pod, or 1 teaspoon real extract

500 ml single cream

Castor sugar for brûléeing, about 1 flat tablespoon per ramekin (to cover with a very thin layer)

Containers
Four individual brûlée ramekins or one shallow ceramic tart dish.

GRANADILLA CURD (FOR TARTS, ICE CREAM, SCONE TOPPING AND MANY MORE APPLICATIONS)

Lemon is the default curd, but there is something about the rounded floral quality of passion fruit that makes a granadilla curd even better. Granadillas are tart, but not straightforwardly so: they contain sulphur compounds similar to those in Sauvignon Blanc wines, which add musky complexity. A curd is as simple to make as a custard (in fact, it is a sort of custard, made with fruit juice in place of milk or cream), and yet curds are rarely made any more. There are so many things to do with a curd: it's brilliant inside a sweet tart crust (sugared and brûléed just before serving, as per the best lemon tarts); wonderful mixed with whipped cream into a fool or topping for a pavlova; and also great blobbed atop a bowl of creamy yoghurt. It's also strangely good on a scone, and perfect stirred into shop-bought vanilla ice cream before freezing the whole mass again. Bottles of the stuff make a beautiful present. In short, it is a jack of all trades and master of every one. This recipe comes from Nigella Lawson's staggeringly useful How to be a Domestic Goddess.*

Place the granadilla pulp in a colander or sieve over a bowl and work about with a spoon to release the juice and pulp. Leave to drain. Reserve the necessary seeds.

Off the heat, beat eggs, yolks and sugar together in a small pot until sugar dissolves. Add granadilla juice and butter. Place pot on lowest heat and stir mixture constantly – and I mean constantly – until it thickens up well. This takes only five minutes or so. Decant into a bowl and leave to cool. If not using the curd on the spot, bottle and store it in the fridge for up to a month.

FOR ONE BOTTLE

Juice from 10 large granadillas, or 14 if small

Seeds from only 2 of the granadillas

2 whole eggs

2 yolks

150 g castor sugar

100 g butter

HOME

I thought it best not to use the word 'comfort' here because it seems nowadays, in a food context, to evoke a particular genre of food, rather than the notion of actual comfort. But even the idea of home is tricky. My idea of homely is probably not going to be yours. Well, obviously not. It's no doubt plain ignorant of me to label chicken yassa a 'homely' Senegalese dish, and many might think Asian salad is a daft inclusion here. But these are things that feel homely to me, at any rate, which is all I have to go on.

Homely food and comfort food (the real kind, not the gastro-pub genre) don't always converge anyway. Unlike many, I see nothing comforting about a plate of lasagne, which is the dish most likely to make me run *away* from home. And one of my ultimate comfort meals is an airline meal, even a terribly bad one, which is probably not about home. Or perhaps it is. Perhaps it's about trying to make a tiny tray-sized bit of homeliness in the sky. Home or away, comfort or otherwise, see this as a selection of dishes that have no lofty ambitions and will not stress the cook.

LAMPEDUSA PIE

CURRIED **MUNG-BEAN SOUP**

Offering comfort and intense flavour at the same time, this is a soup I could eat every day. Somehow, perhaps it's the Indian spicing, it feels exactly right for both summer and winter. This recipe serves eight to ten, but if you make the whole amount, it keeps for days in the fridge and freezes well. The soup keeps thickening if stored in the fridge, so when reheating you need to add a bit more water.

Fry spices in the oil with onion, adding turmeric and garlic last, for a few minutes on a low heat.

Add soaked mung beans and fry for about five minutes. Add the water, salt and tomato paste if using.

Simmer, covered, until mung beans are soft, probably about 30 minutes.

Season and check taste and texture; it should be a loose-ish, dhal thickness. It should have a little sour and sweet behind the spicing, so add sugar and a little lemon juice to taste. Stir in the chopped coriander and butter.

On serving, add a generous blob of full-cream yoghurt, and the toasted cumin seeds. As always, I think chilli is a great extra.

SERVES EIGHT TO TEN

2 tablespoons olive oil

1 tablespoon ground cumin

1 teaspoon coriander

1 teaspoon paprika

1 teaspoon white pepper

1 heaped tablespoon grated fresh ginger

3 cardamom pods

1 cup chopped coriander leaves

2 teaspoons ground turmeric

3 onions, diced small

2 heaped teaspoons slivered garlic

1 kg mung beans, rinsed and soaked for 30 minutes

2 litres water

Salt to taste

1 tablespoon tomato paste – optional

Sugar, lemon juice and extra salt to balance at end

2 tablespoons butter

To serve
Yoghurt, toasted cumin seeds, chilli soaked in oil or fresh chilli

CHICKEN YASSA

From the great book Seductions of Rice, *this is one of West Africa's most famous dishes – and for good reason. This version is from Casamance in Senegal, and is so so so lemony. I mean really quite seriously lemony. If you don't like sour, turn the page.*

You should try to get hold of as free-ranging a bird as possible. Well, you should always steer clear of manky battery chicken (which is pretty much any chicken not marked as free range), but in this recipe it's super-important to have a richly flavoured bird. Traditionally, the whole bird would be used, chopped up into pieces with the bone in. You can do this, or use already portioned pieces, in which case I would use just thighs and drumsticks, which both want long cooking, as opposed to breast, which starts to seize up and become sawdust all too easily.

Put the chicken pieces in a glass or ceramic bowl and cover with the lemon juice. Leave for about an hour, turning occasionally. When you are ready to continue, remove the chicken from the juice, strain the juice and set both aside separately.

Heat the oil in a deep, heavy-bottomed pot. The oil should be about 2 cm deep. When hot, add the chicken, being careful not to splash yourself. Only put in one layer of chicken pieces at a time (you may have to fry in batches). Fry both sides until golden, salting each side at the beginning of its frying with one teaspoon of the salt.

While the chicken is cooking, cut the onions lengthwise in half, then thinly slice lengthwise (i.e. the opposite way to making rings). Remove the chicken pieces and leave to drain. Discard all but three tablespoons of oil from the pot.

Fry the onions on a low heat in the remaining oil until soft and translucent, stirring frequently to stop them sticking and burning.

Put the chicken back into the pot with the onions, plus the reserved lemon juice, water, chillies and thyme. Bring to the boil, then turn down the heat and simmer for about 20 minutes. The sauce should lose enough water to be a loose muddle of onions with only a little free liquid. Carry on cooking if it's too watery. Add the remaining teaspoon of salt about halfway through the cooking.

Just before serving, taste and adjust the seasoning. If the chillies are very hot, the lemons very tart and the onions not too sweet, you may want to balance with a suggestion of sugar. You definitely don't want sweetness – this is not what the dish is about; you just may need to soften any overly sharp or bitter notes.

Serve this with lots – I mean piles – of steamed jasmine rice, and extra chilli if you're that way inclined. You can add the whole lemons left from the squeezing ten minutes before serving to hint at the lemoniness within.

SERVES FOUR TO SIX

1 large chicken – or about 2 kg of pieces, skin on

1 cup fresh lemon or lime juice

About ⅓ cup peanut or vegetable oil

2 teaspoons salt – more to taste if you like

1 kg onions

1 cup water

2 red chillies (use a variety milder than Thai, but if you do use Thai, remove most seeds)

2 sprigs fresh thyme (about 2 teaspoons)

Freshly ground black pepper (black is in the original recipe but I like white here; you choose)

Zest of 1 lemon (optional)

SRI LANKAN **POTATO & MUSTARD CURRY**

Another fantastic dish from Rick Stein's Far Eastern Odyssey. *You can serve it as one of a couple of curries, with stacks of plain long-grain rice nearby. If you use it as the lone curry, a handful of cashews thrown in is a good plan. Please don't be put off by the lengthy ingredient list; the whole deal is very simple to execute. There are a few tablespoons of fish flakes in the original, which I've omitted, as I suspect procuring said fish flakes might put you off making this curry entirely. Also, it works just fine without them. The fish flakes act as both a savoury and salt element, so just add some extra salt to taste near the end.*

Put the potatoes into a pot of cold salted water, bring to the boil and simmer for about 12 to 15 minutes or until tender, but not breaking up. Drain and set aside.

Meanwhile, put the coriander, cumin and fennel seeds into a spice grinder and grind to a fine powder. Coarsely grind the mustard seeds using a pestle and mortar (or processor, but don't turn them to mush).

Heat the oil in a medium-sized pot. Add the onions or shallots and chillies, and fry gently for a few minutes.

Add the pandan, curry leaves, cinnamon and salt, and fry for another minute or so. Add the garlic, ground spices and turmeric, and fry for another minute.

Add the fenugreek seeds (if using), the potatoes, coconut milk, mustard seeds and water, and bring to a simmer. Add extra salt to taste (probably more than you think) and the lime juice, and simmer for about five minutes more.

I quite like this curry thicker than in the original recipe, and I simmer it until it thickens up like vegetable soup, but it's up to you. It's most forgiving, and just as delicious the next day. Eat it for breakfast with the potatoes chopped up and a fried egg on top. Really.

SERVES THREE TO FOUR

500 g small new potatoes (waxy are best)

1½ teaspoons coriander seeds

1 teaspoon cumin seeds

¼ teaspoon fennel seeds

1 tablespoon yellow mustard seeds

3 tablespoons vegetable oil

100 g onions or shallots, halved and thinly sliced

2 to 4 green chillies (depending on type), thinly sliced

Pandan leaf – entirely optional (sometimes available from Asian greengrocers)

10 to 12 curry leaves

10 cm cinnamon stick (no need to measure precisely), broken up into smaller pieces

½ teaspoon salt

25 g garlic, finely chopped (about 1 tablespoon)

½ teaspoon turmeric powder

Pinch fenugreek seeds (no big issue if you leave out)

120 ml coconut milk

200 ml water

1 tablespoon lime juice (or lemon at a push)

AUSTRIAN BUTTERED BREAD DUMPLINGS IN BROTH

These old-fashioned dumplings are indescribably delicious. They're perfect served in a bowl of clear broth (chicken, beef or vegetable), then sprinkled with copious Parmesan and parsley. The fried onion in the dumplings flavours the broth more than you'd expect, giving even vegetable-based broths an almost meaty savouriness.

Dice the bread very small by hand or in a processor to make coarse breadcrumbs about the size of peanuts or larger.

In a pan, cook the onion in the butter slowly until melting and golden, then add the bread and sauté on medium-low until the bread is golden-brown.

Turn into a bowl, add one of the eggs and two spoons of the flour, season and mix well. The mixture should come together when pressed, but not be too sticky.

Add the second egg, or part of it, if the mix seems too dry and crumbly, and extra flour if it's too moist (the type of bread will determine how wet or dry the dough is). You may end up adding both the second egg and extra flour, to even things out again. No stress, the dumpling mix takes it all in its stride.

Form this lumpy mix into golf-ball-sized spheres (smaller won't hurt but bigger will). Drop the dumplings into about 800 ml of gently simmering (not crazily boiling) broth, and cook for about seven minutes. Ladle the broth and dumplings into four bowls, finishing with finely chopped parsley and freshly grated Parmesan.

MAKES DUMPLINGS FOR FOUR GENEROUS BOWLS OF BROTH

150 g day-or-two-old, good-quality bread (Sourdough and ciabatta both work well, but the essential thing is to use a properly made bread from a bakery, and not a supermarket loaf, which has extra gluten and improver in it, and makes for soggy dumplings. I hate to use the word 'artisanal', but that's what you need here.)

50 g butter

1 medium onion, finely chopped

1 to 2 eggs, beaten

2 to 3 tablespoons white bread or cake flour

Salt and white pepper to taste (It seems white pepper has gone out of fashion, but so many dishes — cottage pie, for example — really cry out for white. Here too, black pepper would be so horribly wrong.)

To serve
Parsley, chopped

Parmesan, finely grated

ROAST CHICKEN WITH **BREAD SAUCE**

This recipe is really for the bread sauce. I think you know how to roast a chicken (though I've given my own ideas here). Bread sauce is not popular, and I think it's because it's so horribly executed, or seen as some sort of Christmas duty, rather than approached as the decadent, creamy, clovey concoction it should be. It suffers the same disrespect as porridge. I mean, it's not as though you're making the sauce to be frugal, right? While using up old bread might have been the reason for its invention, that's unlikely to be your impetus for making it nowadays. So let there be more cream, more onion simmered in butter, more cloves and just more of everything that moves it away from prison gruel (though it will still look like prison gruel – that I can't deny). I know my version is somewhat inauthentic, but I promise that pimped bread sauce is nicer than its modest ancestors.

For southern-hemispherers, this is more logically eaten in winter, instead of in its original Christmas position. Along with the chicken, serve many vegetables. Cauliflower, baby cabbage, sweet-sour onions and peas are all very good wallowing in a dollop of bread sauce.

In a thick-bottomed pot, sauté the onion till very soft but not browning. In another small pot, heat the milk and clove-studded onion, and keep simmering with the lid half on, adding more milk if evaporation is noticeable. Cook until there's a strong clovey taste to the milk (about 20 minutes). I keep ground cloves to hand, to add if the whole cloves aren't doing the job. It should be really clovey. Remove the whole onion (and eat in chunks with lots of salt and butter while you cook the sauce), and pour the milk over the sautéed onion.

Add the breadcrumbs, cream and butter, and stir in well. Simmer on a low heat. Add salt and pepper a bit at a time. The texture should be creamy and thick. Add more milk and cream if the sauce is too thick; let it simmer longer if it's a bit thin. This will largely depend on the bread you use. If I'm doing gravy as well, I keep it thick; if it's the only sauce, then thinner.

I think the following steps make the best roast chicken:

Rub generous salt and minimal olive oil all over the chicken.

Place a lemon and a head of garlic in the body cavity. You can choose to squash out the garlic and eat with the chicken, or just use it as oblique flavour.

Roast the bird breast-side down the whole time. Looks odd, but keeps the usually dry breast moist and even succulent, for all the strange people who prefer white meat.

Roast at 200 °C for between an hour and 90 minutes, depending on the size.

I throw soy and chopped flat-leaf parsley into the pan juices if I'm not in the mood for making gravy, in which case serve with boiled potatoes rather than roasted.

SERVES FOUR

2 tablespoons olive oil

1 medium onion, very finely diced

1 cup full-cream milk, plus maybe more

Extra onion with about 5 cloves stuck into it

About 60 g good white bread (fresh or stale), processed to breadcrumbs, but not too fine. (Please note: you cannot, absolutely never, use shop-bought breadcrumbs for this.)

½ cup cream, plus maybe more

1 heaped tablespoon butter

Salt and white pepper to taste (it must be white)

KONIGSBERGE KLOPSE
(POACHED MEATBALLS IN CAPER AND LEMON SAUCE)

Outside of Germany, excluding its immediate neighbours perhaps, the perception of the German eating experience tends to be a bit bratwurst and beerfest-ish. Obviously this is not the case, and food within the country is hugely varied and much unknown. This recipe from northern Germany, Russian in influence, is a quietly sophisticated dish. Describing a meatball dish as 'sophisticated' may seem to be stretching it, but these soft, poached balls, basking in a pale sauce, studded with capers and scented with bay and lemon, are just that.

At home we always ate a much less urbane version of this dish – a nursery rendition, but no worse for its dumbing down. The meatballs were great buxom things and the sauce was always made without the cream or the capers – a good old gravy really. Nice enough in its own way, but this version has an edge that puts it in another bracket. I know cream sauces strike fear into the modern heart. This is not the place to get started on the cholesterol scam, but just know that the cream is really not overwhelming.

Sauté the onions in the butter, covered, until soft and golden. Add the cooked onions and all the remaining meatball ingredients to the bowl with the soaked bread in it. Mix very well.

Moisten hands with water and shape the meatball mix into 12 or so balls (about golf-ball size).

Bring the poaching-liquid ingredients to the boil and simmer, uncovered, for 10 minutes. Reduce heat to low and gently drop in the meatballs. Simmer, uncovered, for about 15 to 20 minutes.

Carefully transfer the meatballs and liquid into a bowl.

To make the sauce, in the same pot, melt the butter over a low heat. Add the flour and mix in, then add the hot poaching liquid bit by bit, stirring non-stop. When you have added most of the liquid, leave to simmer and thicken for a few minutes. Add the capers, lemon juice and cream, then the meatballs and heat through again; if it seems thicker than pouring cream, add the remaining liquid.

Serve with steamed jasmine rice or boiled potatoes. Put extra capers, lemon juice and pepper on the table.

SERVES FOUR WITH A GOOD APPETITE

Meatballs
1 tablespoon butter

1 onion, finely chopped

2 slices fresh white bread without crusts, torn small (preferably not supermarket grade with extra gluten), softened in 1½ tablespoons milk

200 g beef mince (some recipes mix beef with equal amounts of pork and veal and feel free to do this, but for all sorts of reasons I use just beef)

1 anchovy fillet, drained well and chopped fine (optional)

2 tablespoons finely chopped parsley

1 egg

½ teaspoon finely grated lemon rind

½ teaspoon salt and ¼ teaspoon freshly ground white pepper

Poaching liquid
1 litre water, 1 medium onion, peeled and pierced with 2 cloves, 2 bay leaves, 1 teaspoon salt

Sauce
1½ tablespoons butter

1½ heaped tablespoons flour

3 teaspoons capers, drained

2½ tablespoons fresh lemon juice

½ cup sour or regular cream

CHICKEN BAKED WITH CREAM, GARLIC, MUSTARD & THYME

Creamy, saucy things from the oven do smack of bad eighties cooking, I know. The word 'casserole' lurks in the background, and you're even half expecting a tin of creamed mushroom soup or a cup of supermarket mayonnaise to be thrown in there somewhere. Trust me, though, this is just not that sort of dish at all. Creamy it may be, but the mustard, garlic and herbs give it edge, and the way the cream gets all caramelised and burnt around the edges of the pan and on the meat make it as seductive as a pudding.

Preheat the oven to 190 °C. In a small bowl, mix together the garlic, herbs, mustard, olive oil and salt.

Rub the mix all over the chicken. Add the onions, and lay the chicken and onions in a roasting pan large enough for the chicken to form a single layer. Bake uncovered for 20 minutes.

Mix together the wine or stock, cream and sugar, then pour over the chicken. Bake for another 20 minutes, after which time the cream should be golden-brown in places.

I love this with jasmine rice, but boiled potatoes or mash would also be good friends with the dish. And I think it's pretty much compulsory to put a sharp leaf salad on the table.

SERVES SIX

8 garlic cloves, roughly crushed

2 tablespoons fresh thyme leaves

8 bay leaves

4 tablespoons Dijon mustard

1 tablespoon olive oil

1 heaped teaspoon salt

About 12 chicken pieces, thighs and drumsticks only, skin off

2 onions, thinly sliced

100 ml white wine or chicken stock

300 ml cream

1 teaspoon sugar

PERFECT, SIMPLE **ASIAN SALAD**
(WITH MULTIVALENT SESAME DRESSING)

The dressing depends on getting hold of good sesame oil, with a strong, deep, nutty roastedness, but no hint of bitterness (and certainly no hint of oldness).

Put all the dressing ingredients into a jar, or estimate quantities in a bowl, and shake lightly to mix.

Drain the onions from the vinegar (keep the vinegar for future vinaigrettes). Toss all the salad ingredients, bar the sesame seeds, with enough dressing just to moisten. Check taste and add more dressing if necessary. Do this just before serving. Pile in a heap and sprinkle the sesame seeds on top.

SERVES FOUR

1 Spanish onion, very thinly sliced, and left in ½ cup rice or white grape vinegar to turn bubblegum pink – do this anything from an hour to a day before (The longer you leave the onion, the pinker it goes and the more the onion flavour mellows.)

1 cucumber, peeled and sliced into ribbons with a peeler (Peel until you hit the seedy inside part – do not use this part, keep for a rainy day or eat on the hoof.)

1 carrot, peeled and sliced with peeler into ribbons (optional)

2 teaspoons sesame seeds, toasted to golden-brown in a dry pan, while watching like a hawk

For one jar of dressing

⅓ jar best sesame oil

⅓ jar vegetable or grapeseed oil

⅓ jar rice vinegar

Salt to taste (needs to be quite salty)

Honey or golden syrup to taste (about 2 dessertspoons, depending on the sesame oil)

POTATOES BAKED UNDER A BRICK

This is somewhere between the two classics, potatoes Anna and potatoes dauphinoise, but squashed. The bricks are not a gimmick: there is something about the way the potatoes are compressed while baking that makes them especially delicious. A bowlful of this really needs no accompaniment, save some dressed leaves in a second bowl. But it makes a fine upstanding partner to something like grilled chicken or a meat stew. The recipe comes by way of the great Chicago chef Charlie Trotter (a perfectionist to the point of barminess) and his book The Kitchen Sessions. *I've added – to Chef Trotter's horror, no doubt – onions and thyme.*

Preheat the oven to 180 °C.

Brush the bottom and sides of the biggest oven tray with butter. Slice the potatoes very thinly (skin on or off, it's up to you – it works both ways) and place in a large bowl with the cream, salt, pepper, garlic, thyme and onion, and mix well.

Arrange the potatoes and accessories in a vaguely overlapping way in the oven dish, adding any leftover cream from the bowl. Butter the baking paper and lay it on top. Cover with the smaller baking dish, then with the bricks.

Bake for one hour or until the potatoes are tender. Remove bricks, paper, etc., and bake for 30 minutes to brown. Rest for 10 minutes before eating.

SERVES TWO

5 tablespoons melted butter

4 potatoes

3 cups cream

Salt and pepper to grind over

1 garlic clove, very finely slivered

A few sprigs of thyme

1 onion, very thinly sliced

Equipment
2 clay bricks

Baking paper

2 oven trays, one slightly bigger than the other

ALMOST ZIMBABWEAN **CHICKEN IN PEANUT SAUCE**

Chicken and peanut sauce is a combination you'll find scattered over much of Africa, in dozens of different forms. I adore it. For the last 15 or so years, Kin Malebo in Yeoville has made the best chicken–peanut combination imaginable, with smoked chicken, dende oil and ground dried shrimp in the sauce, and sticky fufu made from cassava on the side. It's pretty time-consuming to make this traditional Congolese dish well. Best bet is to go eat the dish there, in which case – if it's in the evening – you should make an effort with your attire or you'll feel very shabby compared to the staggeringly glamorous West African clientele, who pull out all the stops. For making at home, the following slight adaptation of a traditional Zimbabwean chicken–peanut combination is brilliant. Mielie-pap is by far the best accompaniment, though jasmine rice is pretty good too.

Brown the chicken in the oil on all sides, then remove from the pot.

Sauté the onions till transparent, then add the tomato, water, peanut paste (or peanut butter) and chillies. Return the chicken to the pot (the peanut paste may seem lumpy at first, but will amalgamate with the sauce after some cooking).

Simmer on a low heat until the chicken is tender. If the sauce is still very watery, take the heat up a bit and carry on cooking, while stirring, making sure to work around the pot edges (peanuts burn easily).

Once the sauce is slightly thickened – still loose but not watery – add salt to taste, and serve.

SERVES FOUR TO SIX

1 free-range chicken, jointed, or equivalent chicken pieces

2 tablespoons vegetable oil

2 onions, thinly sliced (shallots are often used instead)

3 large tomatoes, peeled and finely chopped

1 litre water

1 cup finely ground roasted peanuts, or peanut butter

3 chillies, finely chopped

Salt to taste

LAMPEDUSA PIE

MIELIE BREAD (aka *MIELIEBROOD*)

What a neglected and wonderful item this is. The great Louis Leipoldt has some strict instructions for it – a take-no-prisoners, purist style, as you might imagine. I know my favourite recipe deviates from his a little by adding egg and flour, but this is the one I like best. The few 'banned' ingredients hold it together more easily, but I don't think they change its essential nature. Though it's called bread, it has neither the function nor the character of any bread I know. Instead, it plays the same role as potatoes, dumplings or something equally damp and starchy might with a stew.

The home-made version doesn't taste anything like the dense tinned, somewhat rubbery, mielie breads you get in supermarkets (though these certainly have a weird charm of their own). It's much lighter, with a far more interesting texture, and brings out a different aspect of the mielies' flavour. I was initially put off by the idea of shucking and mincing the fresh corn, and the whole business of steaming it in a bowl, but I can assure you that it's way quicker than it sounds on paper.

This is best with a pot of nicely liquid stew (lamb bredie perhaps), where the juices and oils are soupy enough to get readily sucked into the 'bread'. A liquid-ish tamatie smoer also works if you're avoiding meat. Mielie bread is at its most delicious just after coming out of the steaming pot, and wonderful reheated in a steamer or in the oven, smeared with butter.

Cut the kernels off the cobs. Mince them in a mincer or processor till fine, but not puréed totally smooth. Mix together with all the other ingredients in a big bowl.

Tip the dough into another bowl that has been well greased (a pudding basin, glass bowl or a small lasagne-type dish) and is small enough to fit into your biggest pot, and has enough space on top to allow the dough to rise an inch or so.

Cover with a mutton cloth-type towel or wax paper and tie tightly with string. Place the bowl in the pot and pour water into the pot until halfway up the sides of the bowl. Put the lid on, bring to the boil and steam gently for two hours. I put two wooden chopsticks between the pot and the bowl to stop the insane rattling that otherwise fills house and brain for the two hours of cooking time.

Watch the water level and top up if necessary.

When cooked, turn the bread out onto a large plate, cut into thick slices and serve immediately with lots of gravy/sauce/meat juices all about.

If your bread is ready before the rest of the meal, turn off the heat and leave it in the steaming bowl until you're ready with everything else. Time-wise, it's quite forgiving.

MAKES ONE MIELIE BREAD, TO FEED FOUR TO SIX WITH STEW

3 cups very fresh green mielies/white maize (around two cobs)

2 free-range eggs

4 teaspoons cake or bread flour

2 teaspoons baking powder

3 teaspoons butter

1 teaspoon sugar

½ teaspoon salt

WARP-SPEED **RICOTTA GNOCCHI**

These are among the most glorious gnocchi you'll ever eat, but with the huge plus that not a single potato need be peeled, cooked or mashed. From start to finish, they take about 15 minutes. Only the sauce might hold things up, but actually they don't need (or want) anything complicated on them. Though they're much lighter in texture than potato gnocchi, the cheese makes them rich, so a starter-sized portion is more than enough.

Mix all the ingredients except for the dredging flour.

Shape into small, roughly spherical balls, about teaspoon-sized. They look more appetising if you can resist rolling them into factory uniformity, and are lighter if handled minimally.

Roll them gently through the flour on the plate so that they are lightly but evenly coated. It's best to roll and coat one ball first and boil it to make sure the ball is holding together. If it breaks up, mix in a little more flour.

Bring to the boil a pot of water. Don't skimp on the cooking water: the flour coating releases starch into the water and the dumplings will become gluey if the starch can't dissipate.

Cook until the gnocchi float to the surface, and remove one by one with a slotted spoon. Serve post-haste with a good sauce — napoletana, sage and brown butter or crushed walnut, plenty of sea salt, herbs and olive oil. You will know what you prefer to pair them with once you've tasted them.

MAKES FOUR PORTIONS

250 g fresh ricotta (The more expensive, very fresh, soft ricotta may need draining in a kitchen cloth lining a colander for a day. If this seems out of the question, reconcile yourself to adding more flour.)

1 egg yolk

¼ to ½ teaspoon sea salt

30 g Parmesan or similar cheese, finely grated

35 to 40 g cake flour (plus extra flour – about ½ a cup – for dredging, spread over a large plate)

SHORT RIB WITH BEER, SHIITAKES & STAR ANISE

A slightly Japanese-style stew (yes, stews are big in Japan – they just didn't export as well as sushi and tempura). It's comforting, but more complex, intense and elegant than the word 'stew' denotes. The beer, soy and shiitake water are cooked down to get the sauce slightly thick, but don't go thinking about words such as 'jus' or 'reduction', as this will give you the wrong idea about the dish. If you can't get short rib – or you're meat-fat-phobic – use something like trimmed chuck or shin. Serve this with mash, plain steamed rice or over potato cakes.

Place shiitakes in a bowl double their volume, and pour boiling water over to cover generously. Place a saucer or side plate on top to keep every bit of mushroom underwater (in Japan they have nifty and beautiful wooden drop-lids for this). Leave for 30 minutes to a few hours. Once soft, remove the stems and place the hoods back in the water.

Heat the oil in a thick-bottomed pot and brown the short-rib pieces on all sides. Add the beer, then the soy and one cup of the shiitake water. Simmer on low with the lid half on until the meat is tender. This could take anything from 90 minutes to two hours. Halfway through, add the star anise. The sauce should have more or less quartered its volume by the end of the cooking.

Add one teaspoon of the sugar, and the vinegar and ginger, and cook for another 10 minutes – with the lid off if the sauce is still watery, on if it is already a thin-syrup consistency. Check the sugar and soy to see if you need more. Let the stew rest for about 10 minutes with the lid on before serving.

SERVES TWO

Handful dried shiitake mushrooms

2 cups boiling water for reconstituting shiitakes

2 tablespoons vegetable oil

500 g beef short rib

⅔ cup beer (I like a dark Guinness style, but a light beer will do, as long as it has body)

½ cup good-quality soy sauce

3 star anise (or ¼ teaspoon caraway seeds)

1 to 2 teaspoons sugar

2 tablespoons rice vinegar

1 dessertspoon slivered ginger

ITALIAN **CHICKPEA & CELERY SALAD**

Once I start eating this, I can't stop. There's something about the sharp crispness of the celery against the fatty Parmesan that keeps you coming back for more. It takes about five minutes to put together and keeps in the fridge for a good few days, making it just about the most useful standby salad you could hope for. Makes a great side dish for grilled meats, and cured meats such as bresaola, coppa and salami, but is also perfect on its own.

Mix everything together. Season with black pepper, and serve with bread and plenty of lemon wedges.

SERVES FOUR

1 can chickpeas (or equivalent of home-cooked)

2 cups Parmesan, shaved (yes, I know it seems a lot – I didn't say this was a diet dish)

2 cups celery stem and some leaves, chopped finely

6 tablespoons good fruity olive oil

2 tablespoons lemon juice

Good coarse salt to taste

Black pepper to season

CELERY LIME & COCONUT SALAD

The strange little book I found this recipe in described it as Turkish. The combination of celery and coconut doesn't seem too Turkish to me (though I'm no expert), but never mind the origin, it works brilliantly. Please try it. There is no doubt that fresh coconut flesh is first prize, but the salad is still excellent with the dried sort, provided you use best-quality thicker-cut fleshy brands, rather than the very fine, horribly dry stuff. Eat this with barbecued chicken, steak, fish or brinjal.

Mix the yoghurt, garlic and lime rind and juice in a bowl. Fold in the celery and coconut. Leave for about 20 minutes to let the flavours meld. Season with salt and pepper, then spoon into a new bowl and top with the chopped celery and parsley leaves.

SERVES TWO TO THREE

4 tablespoons thick, creamy plain yoghurt

2 garlic cloves, finely crushed

Juice and zest of 1 lime

8 celery sticks, grated or very finely sliced, small handful of leaves reserved

Flesh of ½ a fresh coconut, grated, or 1 cup dried coconut strips or shavings

Salt and black pepper to taste

1 teaspoon flat-leaf parsley, roughly chopped

LAMPEDUSA PIE

KOREAN POTATOES

Well, perhaps Koreans-living-in-Cyrildene-East-Johannesburg potatoes. The restaurant where I ate this went by the description of Korean at any rate. I was bowled over by this dish and thought about it often afterwards, but by the time I got to go and quiz the chef about the recipe, the place had closed down. It's an amazing wok fry of grated potato, something like a coming-undone rosti, but with very unrosti-like flavours. Stupendous on its own, but also a great companion to grilled meats, steamed vegetables, or alongside an Asian salad. And I almost forgot, it's also ridiculously good under a fried or poached egg. This is my version, but pretty close, I think, to the original

Get everything assembled, including potential eaters.

Grate the potatoes on the largest grater option (the holes you use for el cheapo cheese sandwiches).

Heat the vegetable oil in a large pan or wok. When almost smoking hot, add the potato, spread it over the base and leave for a few minutes. Toss, and keep tossing, to get the pieces evenly golden and done all over. They may or may not stick together, depending on the degree of flouriness.

Once cooked through but with some bite left — they should not turn to mush — add the cumin, salt, sesame oil and chilli to taste, and mix through.

Plate up and eat post-haste. (Truth be told, I quite like this dish cold and chewy too, but I'm in the minority.)

FOR TWO PEOPLE

4 waxy potatoes — the waxy aspect is important if you want them to do the rosti thing

2 tablespoons vegetable oil

1 heaped teaspoon cumin seeds

Salt to taste (more than you think judicious)

2 teaspoons sesame oil

1 teaspoon chopped green chilli

INDIAN **BREAD SALAD**

Indian-inspired would perhaps be a better description. This recipe comes from wonder-cook Nicole Stich – she of the brilliant recipe blog www.deliciousdays.com. I've adapted it very slightly, more in terms of the method than ingredient-wise. My only main ingredient change is the omission of chickpeas. Feel free to put them back (1 cup cooked chickpeas per four servings); for me, there's enough starch with the bread.

Toss the bread pieces with the olive oil, cumin seeds and garam masala to coat evenly, then fry or bake until golden-brown and crisp (depending on the bread type, you might need less or more oil, just use your judgement). Grind the salt over and toss through.

Put the tomatoes, cucumber, onion (chickpeas if using) and chilli in a big bowl. Add the cooled croutons.

Mix all the remaining ingredients (i.e. the dressing) in a large jug or similar vessel, then pour over the salad and mix well. If you omit the chickpeas you might want to hold back a little of the dressing; taste and see.

Upturn everything onto an enormous plate and scatter with the whole mint leaves. Eat this with caramelised braaied meat or chicken, on top of smashed-up new potatoes or just on its own. Yoghurt is almost essential on the side.

SERVES FOUR

For the bread
250 g naan bread, pita or sourdough, torn or cut up the size of Brazil nuts

5 tablespoons olive oil

1 tablespoon cumin seeds, ground coarsely in pestle and mortar

1 teaspoon garam masala (or your own mix of ground spices)

Sparse grinding of salt

For the salad
300 g cherry tomatoes, quartered

1 cucumber, peeled, deseeded and sliced or chopped roughly

1 Spanish onion, very thinly sliced

1 jalapeño chilli (or Thai with all seeds removed), thinly slivered

5 tablespoons olive oil

2 tablespoons white or red wine vinegar (or lemon juice)

1 flat teaspoon sugar

Salt to taste

Freshly ground black pepper

1 garlic clove, very finely slivered or mashed up

1 loosely packed cup chopped coriander leaves

½ cup mint leaves, torn just before, plus a handful of extra whole leaves

PIZZETTA

Home attempts, in the average electric or gas oven, at matching the coaly, shardy lightness of a wood-fire oven pizza base are plain silly. Though I know that in many parts of Italy the breadier version (made in bakers' electric deck ovens and in homes) is an accepted variation, I'm never really convinced by those creations. They seem too much like a toasted sandwich with the lid off.

This pizza varietal, however – a fried mini-calzone, or pizza pie, if you like – is a thing in its own right, and not the apologetic shadow of something else. It's born and bred for the home cooking pot. A long-time-back Italian boyfriend of mine got this recipe from his nonna, and so simple and delicious was it, that we'd often make it on our month-long camping beach holidays in remote Zululand, where, at the time, the nearest shop was many hours' drive away on slow sand roads, and the only fresh stuff around us was fish still to be caught.

The ingredients for the dough are ideal for such an outing – once made, the dough was happy to sit and prove in the shade while we snorkelled about for hours. A slightly surreal thing to be putting together on a hot African beach perhaps, but sitting in the shade of the jungle bordering that coastline, still cool from the sea, and eating the crusty, oozing little pies the second they came out of the pot wobbling on the gas burner was heaven. They also taste pretty good when you're not camping, I have since discovered.

To make the dough, sift the flour into a large bowl, and mix in the yeast. Make a deep well in the centre and pour the water and olive oil in. Use a wooden spoon to mix everything roughly, then continue with your very own hands.

Sprinkle some flour onto a clean work surface and knead the dough for five to ten minutes, or as long as you can bear it (the more, the better). It should be fairly elastic.

Put the dough ball back into the bowl, cover with a dish towel and leave for a few hours until it has just about doubled in size. No need to find a warm spot, as long as you have some time: the best proving happens at a not-so-warm temperature over a longer period of time (doughs left in the fridge to prove overnight are often the best).

Sprinkle flour on the work surface again.

Divide the dough into golf-ball-sized nuggets or slightly larger, and roll each out into an oval almost as thin as a Marie biscuit. You can use a pasta machine for this if you like – it's very speedy. On one side, spread the tomato base, rain cheese in the centre and dot on optional extras.

Pizza dough
225 g bread flour

7 g sachet yeast

150 ml water, only just warm

2 tablespoons olive oil*

(or use your own pizza-dough recipe; it's the same thing)

For shallow frying
Virgin olive oil or grapeseed oil

(Continued overleaf)

Make sure to leave a bit of a border with no filling, for easy closing. Wet one side of the dough, fold it over into a half-moon and press together; crimping the edges ensures a good seal.

Pour the oil* into a thick-bottomed pan to about one finger deep. Heat the oil to a point where the dough forms a gentle ring of bubbles when it touches the oil. Don't let it get anywhere near hot enough to smoke. Slide the pizzette into the oil, perhaps two at a time, depending on the size of your pan. They should have plenty of space around them. Fry until golden-brown. These must be eaten without delay, so the nicest way to have this meal is for everyone to gather in the same room as the cook and scoff them as they come off the stove.

If you're not in the middle of Zululand, serve with plainest leaf salad.

* Please do not use Pomace olive oil. It is the dog of the olive oil world (and not a ribboned lapdog or a sleek police hound, but a mangy cur). This oil is extracted by means of high heat and chemicals, just as average supermarket sunflower oil is, tasting of little but still pretty pricey, so you may as well buy el cheapo vegetable oil and know what you're dealing with.

FOR ABOUT SIX PIZZETTE

Filling

Tomato base: Use a really thick tomato base. It's crucial that the base is less liquid than usual – in an open pizza, a watery base loses its moisture to the dry oven air, but enclosed in a sealed dough 'pie', excess moisture is disastrous. Make a standard napoletana sauce and reduce to about half the usual volume. The consistency should be like very thick ketchup.

Cheese: This is the one time when you don't want to use real mozzarella – genuine mozzarella leaks too much moisture. You need cheese grated from those blocks of pale yellow stuff hilariously and outrageously called 'mozzarella' in supermarkets, but actually closer to a long-lost cousin of Gouda. It's not bad-tasting cheese, it's just not mozzarella. Anyway, this mixed with good Parmesan works best.

Garlic: Sliced freshly into paper-thin slivers (not chopped). Use the *Goodfellas* patented razor blade method if you have no knife sharp enough.

Finely slivered onion

Optional fillings: These must be tiny, intense things that don't add too much lumpiness, as this could break the dough casing when still raw. Fresh herbs, anchovies, olives, capers and chilli are all great. Thinly sliced artichoke pieces or salami at a push.

THREE-HOUR **ENGLISH RICE PUDDING**

I don't think there's anything that manages to straddle nursery comfort and luxurious indulgence in quite the way that a slow-baked creamy rice pudding does.

There are merits in pot-stirred rice puddings (think of them as sweet risottos), but what the hours-long baked version has – and this is why you must never dream of taking short cuts – is the caramelly depth, which is really the formation of a sort of dulce de leche. *Time alone can conjure this sort of flavour.*

I like this paired with some nicely sour, proper apricot jam or berry compote. Sour-cherry compote, boozy or teetotal, is also brilliant. And I think it's really best as a meal in its own right. You want to be fully hungry for this – to take the edge off your rice-pudding lust would just be a shame. If you're offering this to visitors rather than making it as a Sunday-evening couch supper (my preferred role for it), and feel you must offer something before, then a bowl of plain leaf salad will be enough. If eating this pudding doesn't make you happy, then I fear there might not be anything that can.

Preheat the oven to 140 °C. If you suspect your oven of being an over-heater (and they're all over or under a little bit), then err on the side of lower temperature.

Put the rice, 700 ml of the milk, the butter, sugar and salt into a baking dish with a 20 cm diameter (or equivalent in squareness). Stir to spread things vaguely evenly, and bake for an hour.

Add the remaining milk, and bake for another hour. By the end of this hour there should already be a golden skin forming.

Lastly, add the cream, pouring around the edges so as not to break up the skin too much.

Bake for a final hour, or until there is a golden-brown blistering crust on the top and the mixture has thickened.

Serve steaming hot with jam, berry compote, baked apples or on its own. If eating this pudding doesn't make you happy, then I fear there might not be anything that can.

SERVES FOUR TO SIX

75 g pudding rice (sushi rice is perfect, or a similar short grain, but not risotto rice)*

1 litre full-cream milk (please don't bother making this with skimmed milk)

30 g unsalted butter, diced

45 g white or castor sugar

Generous pinch salt

150 ml pouring cream (again, using bizarre products such as fat-reduced cream will not work here)

* It might seem that this is too little rice, but don't be tempted to add more, as it swells massively.

ST CLEMENTS PUDDING

If pressed to choose my all-time favourite sweet thing – in a gun-to-the-head scenario – this baked pudding would have to be it. The original name for the pudding, Lemon Delicious, is too terrible (only one step up from Lemon Surprise), but forget names and just make it. It's gloriously tart, light-as-air-yet-totally-comforting wonderment.

There are dozens of versions, but this one from Australian legend Stephanie Alexander is particularly good. I've changed her fine recipe though, by adding orange rind – that way you get both sharpness and fragrance. If you want to make it plain lemon, just leave out the orange rind. You could also use naartjie juice instead of lemon, in which case it tastes wonderfully like Clifton (you remember – the powdered drink we loved as children?).

This is a pudding that feels equally at home as part of a Sunday-night comfort supper in one container, and as a swanky dinner ending, cooked and served in individual ramekins. Perhaps with some pouring cream on the side?

Preheat the oven to 180 °C.

Cream the butter, sugar and zest, by hand with a big wooden spoon, or in a processor. Add the yolks, then flour and milk alternately to make a smooth batter. Mix in the lemon juice.

Beat the egg whites until you have firmish (but not dry) peaks and fold them into the batter. It may well look curdled now – do not despair, this is its way.

Pour the curdly mass into two well-buttered 500 ml dishes or a one-litre dish.

Stand the dish(es) in a deep roasting tray or similar, place this tray in the oven, then fill the tray to halfway up the side(s) of the pudding dish(es) with boiling water.

Bake at 180 °C for around 30 minutes for the smaller dishes or 40 minutes for the single larger dish, or till a deep golden on top, and a somewhat wobbly, but not liquid, interior. You should have a crusty top and an oozy saucy bottom. Eat scaldingly hot.

SERVES TWO

3 tablespoons butter

250 ml cup castor sugar (1 cup)

Finely grated zest of 1 lemon

Finely grated zest of ½ an orange (optional but recommended)

3 eggs, separated

3 tablespoons self-raising flour

375 ml milk

Juice of 1½ lemons

GUAVA COBBLER

Guavas are underused. I know that they're not actually indigenous fruit, but they feel so much like ours. And they're one of those fruits that behave so well in a tin that, as with pears, using tinned instead of fresh gives you just as delicious a result. The cobbler topping also works brilliantly with berries, apples or pears.

This cobbler is very close to the one we used to have for high-school lunches. The main courses were always grey, tasteless messes of pottage (with the so-called cottage pie a real prison-grade low point), but the kitchen got it impressively right with the puddings. We could never have enough of them, signing up for hot lunches every term only so we could get these end morsels.

We were served this with custard, but if you don't feel up to making the stuff, pouring cream is just as wonderful an addition.

Heat the oven to 200 °C.

Place the guavas in a baking dish and scatter over the muscovado sugar and the 30 g butter in pieces.

Rub the flour, baking powder and the 100 g butter together until fine breadcrumbs, no more.

Stir in the cream and two tablespoons of the plain or castor sugar with a fork until just combined.

Shape the dough into blobby scone-like masses about a centimetre thick, and place on the fruit to cover evenly but don't worry about leaving gaps.

Sprinkle with the remaining tablespoon of sugar.

Bake for 40 minutes, reducing the heat to 180 °C when you put the cobbler in the oven.

Let your cobbler rest for a few minutes before eating.

SERVES FOUR TO FIVE AS A PUDDING, TWO TO THREE AS SUNDAY SUPPER

5 fresh guavas, peeled and poached for 30 minutes in bought apple or grape juice and drained; or one 450 g tin guavas, drained

2 to 3 tablespoons light muscovado sugar

30 g butter, cut into small pieces

225 g plain flour

1½ teaspoons baking powder

100 g chilled unsalted butter

170 ml cream

3 tablespoons plain or castor sugar

BEST-EVER **MELKTERT**

That's what the 1987 Huisgenoot Winning Recipes Cookbook *called this recipe, and, yes, it is. I've been searching for a perfect melktert recipe for so so long, and have been disappointed by so many. A perfect melktert (and I've checked with my Afrikaans friends, so it's not just my waspy thoughts on the matter), should be just set, so that cutting a neat slice with sides that remain primly vertical is almost impossible. This one equals the best I've ever had (which happened to be, very rightly, at the tea shop at the Voortrekker Monument). Thank you, Mrs Elbe Esterhuizen of Johannesburg, for this wobblesome glory.*

The pastry here is very good – tender and puffy, as it should be (quite unlike a 'normal' sweet shortcrust), but I think you could even skip the pastry and just make the silken filling, which is blissful eaten like a pudding from little ramekins.

Start with the pastry. Butter a large pie dish, either square or round (30 cm diameter or 30 cm square), or two smaller ones. I like to use a dish you can serve from – something not too depressing-looking – because it's virtually impossible to transfer the tart, as a whole, while fresh. Mix the butter and sugar, then add the egg and mix well. Sift in the flour, baking powder and salt, and mix all together well, but lightly. Leave to rest for 30 minutes to an hour.

Preheat the oven to 200 °C. Thinly line the base and sides of the pie dish with the pastry by cutting off slices and pressing them onto the pie dish. Neaten the edges if you object to the rustic look. Leave to rest again for about 10 minutes in the fridge. You can make the base long before and leave it covered in the fridge for days.

Prick the pie shell all over with a fork and bake for about 10 minutes or until golden.

While it's baking, start the filling. Separate two of the eggs. Beat together the cream, the whole egg, two yolks, and the sugar, flour, cornflour and salt to a paste in a large bowl. Bring the milk and butter to the boil in a large pot.

Gradually mix half the boiled milk into this paste, then pour all of this back into the mix, keeping it at a simmer, and whisking all the time to stop lumps from forming.

Once thickened, keep on the lowest heat while you beat the two egg whites until soft-peak stage, and fold well into the hot milk mixture.

Pour the filling into the baked pastry shell(s), sprinkle lavishly with cinnamon, and leave to cool until the filling has set. This will take a good few hours.

MAKES FOUR PORTIONS

Pastry

125 g butter (Mrs Esterhuizen gives the option of margarine, but here I must part company with her)

100 g sugar

1 egg, beaten

275 g cake flour

10 ml baking powder

Generous pinch of salt

Filling

3 eggs

125 ml cream

150 g white sugar

20 g cake flour

20 g cornflour

Pinch of salt

1 litre milk

25 g butter

Cinnamon to sprinkle on top

CRUSTLESS **LEMON & NAARTJIE CHEESECAKE**

If I had to choose only one cheesecake type, then the buxom German cheesecakes I grew up with – lemony, quite dense, with that charred, almost tough, top layer – would win hands down. This sort of cheesecake was the one and only type served in all the continental cafes peppering Hillbrow up until I was in my late twenties. Strange, quiet, carpeted places filled with big brown leather chairs, Eiffel Tower replicas and old men playing backgammon. What the attraction was for us as teenagers I'm not too sure. Perhaps it was just the cheesecake…

This recipe comes close to these sturdy ones in flavour, but is a bit lighter and fluffier, thanks to the beaten cream. Also, because I've removed the crust at the bottom, I've added a topping of uncooked citrusy cream cheese for some texture play. I don't like the way crust interferes with the smoothness of cheesecake filling, but obviously feel free to add your own crust if you can't imagine cheesecake without it. I've added naartjie rind to the topping because it's so fragrant, but you can leave it out if you like. If you use fat-free cream cheese, the cake might take longer to cook, and be a bit watery on cutting. Try not to use anything but full cream.

Preheat the oven to 150 °C.

Beat the cream cheese and sugar together until totally smooth and amalgamated.

Add the eggs one by one, then the vanilla, cornflour or rice flour and lemon juice, beating all in well.

In a clean bowl, beat the cream until thick – almost stiff peaks. Watch closely all the time. There is nought as easy to mistakenly do, or as impossible to reverse, as cream that goes into the almost-butter stage. Fold the cream into the cream cheese mix and pour into a greased and lined spring-form cake tin and bake for 50 minutes.

Leave the cake to cool completely – this means for at least three hours.

Mix all the topping ingredients together and spread evenly over the cake.

It keeps for about four days in cool weather, two to three in warmer.

I have a slightly perverse desire for hot cheesecake. Or maybe not so perverse – it's a bit like a blintz without the filling. I can't recommend it highly enough. It induces a brief stomach ache, but is well worth the discomfort. Of course, if you cut a slice from the hot cake the whole thing collapses, so a good idea whenever you bake this cake is to fill one ramekin (a crème brûlée-type container) with a bit of the filling, which you remove at the half-hour mark and scoff immediately with some cold cream or cold berry compote.

SERVES ABOUT EIGHT

725 g thick cream cheese

150 g castor sugar

5 eggs

1 teaspoon vanilla extract

45 g rice flour or cornflour

40 ml lemon juice

300 ml cream

Topping

Rind of 1 lemon and 1 naartjie, finely zested

2 tubs full-cream cream cheese

2 tablespoons castor sugar

SCONES & THEIR WAYS

Scones. How I feared them when I was young. There we'd be, at a tea-time affair at someone's house, and the mom would disappear to fetch 'The Plate'. I would wish so hard that it might arrive bearing chocolate cake, gingerbread, even Marie biscuits – not thrilling, but at least reliable. The mom would return, and if it was scones, how we shook in our boots. We'd had them before and we knew this time would be no different. Also, we understood that we couldn't say no. This was long before the convenience that wheat allergies and other such food sensitivities have bestowed on unwilling eaters. In 1975 or thereabouts, there could be no feasible excuse for refusing a food item that other humans happily scoffed.

One bite and our fears were almost always confirmed: the scones would be stolid, dry and friable in that way that makes it pretty much compulsory to take a giant gulp of liquid with every bite, to get the thing down. The combination of scone dryness and a throat tickle brought on by the merry party of chemicals in what was invariably Oros, was not what tea-time dreams are made of.

Of course if more love had gone into the toppings all might have been bearable, but more often than not, you were confronted by a scraping of margarine and a miserly central little drop of bad jam. Could it get worse? Yes: no cream. Oh, these were very mean scones indeed. Even when we fed ours to the dog while no one was looking, the scone was not our friend. So dry and unwieldy in the mouth was the bad scone that even the dog couldn't manage it without a battle. We'd watch in horror as every dog-spit-enrobed crumb cluster did a slow-motion spray from his champing lips, spreading the evidence further over the hostess's stoep (always, in my memory, a blindingly sunny, flaking slasto stoep). Ja, those terrible scone days.

Cut to many years later in high-school home-economics class, where one fine day scones were the chosen task, and biting into my oven-fresh creation, a moment of scone-jouissance ensued. I was agog – confused even. How had I not known this before? It was not scones that were the problem, it was neglected stale scones, and scones that were doomed from birth by bad recipes. Obviously, good scones are profoundly delicious. Better than many cakes, really.

This is my favourite scone recipe. It uses yoghurt or buttermilk, which makes a very tender scone. Traditionalists may mock the use of self-raising flour in place of plain flour plus raising agent, but I think the results are better. Please serve these with the best butter, jam and cream you can get hold of (double-thick or Jersey cream is best).

Preheat the oven to 200 °C.

Line a large baking tray with baking paper or grease well with butter. Sift the flour into a large bowl. Add the salt and butter, and rub with your fingers until the mixture is like lumpy sand. Be light and quick – don't work it to death. Lightness is the keyword with scones, and must be applied in both the mixing and the rolling.

Mix in most of the yoghurt or buttermilk, adding more liquid or flour if the mix seems too sticky or too dry. It should be soft and damp, and just firm enough to keep its shape.

500 g self-raising flour

1 teaspoon salt

125 g unsalted butter (or salted butter and leave out the salt)

About 300 ml good-quality plain yoghurt (or buttermilk)

1 egg plus 1 tablespoon milk, beaten together, for egg wash

(Continued on page 86)

Stop mixing as soon as the dough holds together, and pile onto a floured surface. Roll or press until about two fingers thick.

Cut out the scones, dipping the cutter into flour between each one. Re-roll the rest of the dough and cut the remaining scones. A note about the scone cutter: don't use a jam jar, as trapping and compressing the air forces the scone dough to be a little compressed in the process too. It must be a proper cutter.

Place on the baking tray and brush liberally with the egg yolk and milk mix. I know the use of one egg, which will only get half-used, is frustrating; if it irks you too much, just use milk. Two scone aficionados tell me that it's imperative to put the scones close together on the baking tray to stop them flattening out as they cook.

Bake for about 10 minutes, or until golden on top. The exact timing will be different for every oven. The first batch, for better or worse, must be your litmus test and guide for all further scone forays. Once out, break open one scone immediately, spread with copious butter and eat while still scaldingly hot, then cover the rest lightly with a thin napkin and serve post-haste.

MAKES ABOUT 10 SCONES, DEPENDING ON YOUR CUTTER

TOFFEED **APPLE CRUMBLE**

Apples want to be with caramel. Or toffee. Or fudge. Or whatever word you use to describe the indescribably deep resonance that comes from browned sugar, the umami *of the pudding world. The use of treacle sugar is really a massive cheat, but the end result is so good that I think you'll be able to live with yourself.*

Rub the butter into the flour until you have peanut- and walnut-sized bits. Remember that a good crumble is a coarse one. Mix in the sugar. Refrigerate until needed. (If it makes you feel a bit better about the high sugar, high fat and refined flour, substitute half the flour with oats. It's just as good.)

Mix the apples with the orange juice. Pour the apples and juice into a 20 cm ceramic pie dish or ovenproof bowl (you could also divide the mix among smaller bowls for individual servings).

Dot the 1½ tablespoons of butter evenly over the apples, and sprinkle the cinnamon and treacle sugar over all. Scatter the crumble over the apples.

Bake at 180 °C for about 30 minutes, or until the crumble is golden.

Serve immediately with pouring cream, ice cream or custard.

SERVES TWO TO THREE

Crumble

65 g cold butter, cubed

90 g self-raising flour (I know plain flour is traditional, but actually self-raising is better.)

4 tablespoons light brown sugar

Filling

4 small or 3 big apples, peeled, cored and sliced thickly

Juice of 1 small orange

Bold dash of cinnamon

1½ tablespoons butter

2 tablespoons dark treacle sugar (the sticky one. It must be this sugar and no other, I'm afraid.)

PARTY

All sensible people know that actually any dish on earth is fit for a party. It all depends on the party, doesn't it? These are just recipes that say 'enormous table and lots of people' to me, because they are very happy-looking dishes, or want to be made in monumental volumes, or have the sort of intensity and punch that suit party mode. The best recipe for a good party is in fact the following: a fantastic cocktail, volumes of whatever food you've made (your friends would rather have enough lentil soup than not enough crayfish, especially if they're drinking) and no Modern Talking in the music mix.

ZUCCHINE FRITTE (DEEP-FRIED BABY MARROW)

When I first tried this at the wonderful Italian restaurant Assaggi in Johannesburg, it seemed such a modern sort of dish, but then I discovered through Elizabeth David, bless her (undoubtedly 100 per cent) cotton socks, that it's been a traditional snack item in Italy for just about ever.

Follow everything to the letter, and you have the most delicious slivers of crisp vegetable chips. Deep-fried though this is, it doesn't feel heavy in the least. I like it on its own as a pre-lunch thing, just put out the way you would peanuts, or as part of a small meze-ish affair.

Cut the zucchine into strips about shoestring-chip size. Toss evenly with salt and leave in a colander in the sink to drain for no less than 45 minutes. You can leave them for as long as two hours.

Rinse off the salt and drain again well, even pressing lightly between tea towels if in a rush.

Dredge thoroughly and evenly with flour. Tossing them together in a plastic bag with the flour is the least messy way and uses the least flour.

Shake off excess flour and deep-fry until light golden, but *not brown*.

Drain on paper towels and serve immediately. Lemon juice squeezed over just nano-seconds before eating is very nice but not essential (and not advisable unless all the zucchine are going to be eaten within minutes of applying the juice).

FOR FOUR PEOPLE, DEPENDING ON ACCOMPANIMENTS

About 800 g baby marrow (the smaller and greener, the better; those left to get too large, and turning a paler yellowy green – teen marrows – are not what you want)

60 g coarse salt

250 g cake or bread flour and 50 g cornflour

Vegetable oil (although I bet duck fat would be brilliant)

DEVILS ON HORSEBACK

Why don't we serve this any more? I can't imagine – it's a perfect example of how much pork loves sweet. Streaky bacon is wrapped around pitted prunes and baked until the prunes are oozy and the bacon crisping but still juicy. Serve it as a hand-around (dare I say canapé?) before lunch or supper, or as a sit-down thing, dotted about a vinaigrette-dressed leaf salad. You can't imagine how happily salty-fatty pork, sweet prunes and sharp leaves sit together.

Preheat the oven to 200 °C.

Wrap a rasher of bacon around each prune. If you can't find nice big plump ones, use two per bundle, i.e. double up on the prunes. Fasten with a toothpick in whatever way seems sensible. Lay them on a baking tray and bake until the bacon is crisping and browning. Serve immediately.

SERVES ABOUT FOUR (JUDGE THE CROWD)

16 large, juicy pitted prunes (double-check that they are pitted: it's emergency dental appointments if you don't)

16 rashers streaky bacon (no other bacon will do: you need the fat, and it wraps obediently)

16 toothpicks (if you don't like the look of them or the associations, take them out before serving)

LEMON-PARMESAN-**CHILLI BREAD**

A fantastic variation on classic garlic bread. I know what you're going to say: if it's not broken, don't fix it, right? But don't think of this version as an uncalled-for mess-about with a classic. Rather see it as a perfect concoction in its own right. The recipe also comes from gifted German lass Nicole Stich, author of the site www. deliciousdays.com, one of the best food blogs in existence.

Chop all the vegetable matter finely, then mix all the filling ingredients together.

Slice the baguette as you would for making garlic bread, and spread the filling thickly and evenly between the slices.

Wrap the bread in baking paper – or foil failing that – and bake for about 15 minutes at about 180–200 °C. Eat immediately, with black olives, or alongside a traditional braai meal.

This butter is also good spread onto pieces of ciabatta or sourdough bread, which are put under the grill. And a round of this butter is just fantastic placed on top of a steak upon serving, or smeared onto big black mushrooms before roasting them in the oven.

FOR ONE BAGUETTE (SERVES ABOUT FOUR)

½ green chilli, seeds removed

1 shallot or onion

1 clove garlic

¼ cup chives

125 g soft-enough-to-mash butter

2 tablespoons olive oil

Grated rind of 2 lemons

50 g good-quality Parmesan, grated

Sea salt and black pepper to taste

1 baguette

BEETROOT & ORANGE SOUP

I know. Beetroot – so many haters. Why, I'm not sure. What I do know is that this soup has converted many hardened anti-beetrooters. I think the orange cuts through the soiliness, which is perhaps what most beet-detesters fear. You can serve it hot or very well chilled. I prefer hot.

Heat the oil in a thick-bottomed pot, and sauté the onion very slowly until it is softening but not browning. Meanwhile, chop the beetroot coarsely, add it to the pot and sauté for a minute or two.

Add the water or stock and simmer, half-covered, on the lowest heat for 30 minutes or until the beetroot is soft. Cool slightly and put everything through a blender. The degree of smoothness is up to you.

Pour back into the pot and reheat, while adding most of the orange juice and rind, plus salt and sugar to taste.

Let the flavours come together for a few minutes, then add the remaining orange if you think it needs it, and balance sweet and salt again (if serving hot, you'll most likely need less sweet, more salt, and vice versa if serving cold).

Add a dollop of sour cream or crème fraiche on serving, plus chopped chives and black pepper. With the hot version, good bread on the side – kitka, sourdough or pretzel bread – is a necessity. If buttered, even better.

SERVES SIX

2 tablespoons olive oil

200 g onion, coarsely chopped

500 g freshest best beetroot – firm and brightly coloured

1 litre water or stock (chicken or beef)

Juice and rinds of 2 oranges

Sugar and salt to taste (the amounts depend very much on whether you've used stock or water, whether the beetroot was very fresh and sweet, and the relative sweetness or tartness of the oranges)

NOT-GAZPACHO (aka RAW VEGETABLE SOUP)

I don't like gazpacho – classic tomato gazpacho, that is. I suspect that, as with most food dislikes, childhood trauma is to blame.

In the white suburban Joburg of the seventies, most of our moms were smitten by the combined exoticness and ease of the Spanish classic. They took to it so gleefully that for a good few years every second invitation out meant wading through a bowl of the stuff before you could get your hands on anything solid. That might have been all right, but somehow in the hands of our not so Latino moms, the point of the dish got lost in translation. Their less than Spanish boldness in the seasoning, the not-enough-time-left-for-chilling syndrome, and the grown-for-size-not-flavour beef tomatoes, which were all that the greengrocers stocked then, meant that the resulting gazpacho was usually a bowl of tepid, slightly salty, floury tomato mash – an uncooked napoletana sauce, almost.

To this day, raw mashed tomato is plain disgusting to me, which is why I came up with this version of the soup when I had my first restaurant, Superbonbon. It has little to do with the principles of true gazpacho, though it does have the raw thing going on. It's just delicious, and I think more refreshing than the tomato concoction.

Serve this as a starter topped with black pepper, yoghurt and toasted sesame seeds, or on a really hot day, as a main course with all of the above, plus the best croutons, served separately.

You can alter the ratios of the vegetables and herbs quite radically – it's the general idea of chilled, green, sharp and fresh that counts.

Blend everything in batches, with some vegetable matter and some water in each batch, until you have a not entirely smooth mix. Adjust the consistency with more water if needed, and, lastly, adjust the seasoning.

Unless all the ingredients were well chilled when blended, chill for at least two hours, and up to 12 hours ahead.

Side items
Use full-cream or double-cream yoghurt, as the soup itself is so lean. Coconut milk instead of the yoghurt is very good too.

Don't skip the toasting of the sesame seeds. Without this step, they taste like nothing. Put them into a dry, hot pan and toss about, watching all the time. They burn mighty easily.

SERVES EIGHT

3 cucumbers, peeled and roughly chopped

4 avocados

2 green peppers, pips removed

1½ cups spring onion

4 teaspoons fresh ginger

¾ cup lemon juice

6 teaspoons white sugar (or to taste)

½ cup chopped coriander

4 cups water (or enough to make a thick soup)

1 flat teaspoon salt (or to taste)

1 teaspoon freshly ground black pepper

LAMPEDUSA PIE

TOMATO-CHILLI-GINGER RELISH

A punchy, lightning-quick hot relish (I don't know what else to call it; it's not a sauce, a chutney or a pickle), which is brilliant poured over grilled chicken, halloumi or fish. It's so simple that it's more a notion than a recipe – you can just scan the ingredients and feel your way.

Heat the oil in a thick-bottomed pan and fry the ginger and chilli on a high heat until they start getting soft. Add the tomatoes and keep frying on a high heat until they're caramelising in places, but not turning to mush. Add the sugar and salt, adjust to taste, and eat while hot (the amount of sugar depends on the sweetness of the tomatoes and the heat of the chilli, probably about a teaspoon or so; add less and taste as you go).

FOR TWO

2 tablespoons olive oil

1 tablespoon slivered ginger

1 teaspoon chopped Thai chilli, deseeded

1 cup ripe baby Roma tomatoes, cut in half

Sugar to taste

Flake or sea salt, ground, to taste

ALEPPO-STYLE BABA GHANOUSH

The baba ghanoush I've always known and made is the fairly smooth one composed mainly of brinjal (aubergine). This version, which actually bears little relation to the former, is made in the Aleppo region of Syria. The recipe comes from Silvena Rowe's magical Orient Express. It's sharp, smoky, mega-savoury, and wants to be dolloped on top of so many things that the danger is you start using it as a ketchup of sorts. Because it's not a purée, it functions as both a sauce and a salad. Grilled chicken, steak, lamb, fish and roasted vegetables all seem to cry out for it. Halloumi cheese, too, yearns to be slathered with the stuff. And obviously, it's brilliant on bread.

The ultimate way is to cook the brinjals over coals, which imparts a smoky flavour, but it's more realistic to cook them in the oven, and the dip is almost as delicious. Slice and oil the brinjals, and roast at 200 °C until soft but not mushy – about 30 minutes.

When cooked, dice the brinjals small and mix them with all the remaining ingredients. Only add the salt just before serving so that the juices don't drain from the tomato and form a soggy lake.

SERVES FOUR TO SIX

2 large brinjals

1 tablespoon ground cumin

1 small green pepper, deseeded and finely chopped

1 small onion, finely chopped

1 ripe tomato, finely chopped

1 garlic clove, smashed and mashed or very finely sliced

Small bunch flat-leaf parsley, finely chopped

Juice of 1 lemon

Salt to taste – only on serving

50 g walnuts, roughly chopped (optional)

PARSLEY & SPANISH ONION SAUCE (FOR WHITE ANCHOVIES AND A LOT OF OTHER THINGS TOO)

White anchovies are unutterably delicious served on toast (if it's Italian bread, call it crostini if you like), and topped with a big dollop of this oily, raw concoction. Unlike salted anchovies, which are far more intense and fishy, white anchovies pickled in wine vinegar (usually) are closer to a pickled herring in flavour – mild and with a silky texture. They usually go by their Spanish name boquerones *in delis.*

The same sauce – or dressing perhaps – is also fantastic with grilled calamari or fish, braaied lamb and over white cheeses such as mozzarella, halloumi and labneh.

The sauce should be mixed about 15 minutes before using to let the flavours come together, but no more than a few hours before. You can use normal onions if no Spanish ones are about, but the taste is softer with Spanish, and the sauce more beautiful.

For me, it's even better with a tiny bit of chilli in the sauce, but I tend to think this about almost everything except pudding, so perhaps just put this on the side.

Mix all the sauce ingredients together and set aside.

Toast or grill the bread, top sparsely with the anchovies and dollop the sauce generously and evenly over the pieces. Grind some black pepper over everything, and plonk lemon wedges and lots of herbs on the plates.

If serving with grilled meats or fish, pass the sauce round for everyone to add their own.

SAUCE TO DRESS ANCHOVIES FOR FOUR

2 tablespoons flat-leaf parsley, chopped finely

1 tablespoon grated or zested lemon rind

2 tablespoons Spanish onion, chopped finely

Sea salt/flake salt to taste – remember, the fish is somewhat salty too

Enough olive oil to cover the ingredients well

8 thin slices good ciabatta or sourdough bread

About 6 pieces white anchovies in oil

Black pepper

Lemon wedge, and herbs to serve (I like rocket and watercress)

HOT, SHARP **HERB DRESSING**

As the name says, very chilli, very sour, very herby. Also, a little bit sweet and perhaps somewhat Vietnamese. This dressing (or sauce or dip or marinade) is just the most delicious thing to throw over grilled fish, chicken, a rare rib-eye steak, lamb chops or wokked calamari, either before or after cooking. Lovely with duck breast too. And roasted brinjal (aubergine). Also fantastic with steamed rice and rice noodles. Yes, really, all those things. It keeps in the fridge for a good few weeks, but will only look as verdant as the picture on the first day (the vinegar strips the colour out of the greens).

Throw everything into a bottle or bowl and mix. Check the sweet-sour-hot-salt balance, and adjust if need be. This will depend a lot on the type of chillies you use and whether you remove the seeds. More sweet and more salt are needed if the chillies are very hot.

Store in the fridge.

MAKES ONE SMALL BOTTLE

100 ml cider or rice vinegar

2 tablespoons white sugar

1 teaspoon fresh ginger, finely slivered

½ teaspoon garlic, finely slivered

1 teaspoon red or green chilli, finely sliced

6 teaspoons mix of some or all of the following: coriander leaves, mint leaves, small spring onion, all chopped or sliced finely

1 teaspoon fine lemon or lime zest

1 tablespoon top-quality fish sauce

WALNUT & PISTACHIO DRESSING FOR GREEN SALAD (AND OTHER THINGS)

This dressing – another find from the brilliant blog deliciousdays.com – is so good you want to drink it straight from the container. Apart from its obvious use mixed into a big bowl of leaves, it's also good poured over hot, boiled potatoes, in a classic eighties-type spinach and bacon salad, or with roast chicken.

Grind the nuts to a rough rubble in a grinder or processor. Don't, whatever you do, let them turn into powder. Combine the nuts with the remaining ingredients, check for balance of salt, sweet and sour, and adjust as necessary.

SERVES TWO

12 walnut halves

1 heaped tablespoon unsalted shelled pistachios

6 tablespoons fruity olive oil

2 tablespoons honey

1 tablespoon white wine vinegar

FENNEL, CHILLI & CUCUMBER SALAD
(FOR BRAAIED AND GRILLED MEATS AND FISH)

This is almost my favourite salad in the world to accompany any coal-charred, caramelised meaty items. It's not bad on its own either, but to come into its own, it really wants the oily smokiness of the meat. If you don't eat meat or fish, braaied or grilled brinjals or mushrooms, lavishly brushed with olive oil, would go some way to getting the same effect.

Mix the oil, lemon, salt, chilli and mint. In a large bowl, toss with the cucumber and fennel, and decant into a serving bowl or plate. Add the dressing just before serving.

Use any leftover (now pale and soggy) salad to stuff into a fat white roll along with leftover meat, for an excellent supper sandwich (for some reason, I tend to picture this salad being served at lunch).

FOR TWO (INCREASE AS NECESSARY)

5 tablespoons best olive oil

2½ tablespoons lemon juice

Flake salt to taste

1 or 2 red chillies, all seeds removed and very finely sliced

1 heaped tablespoon mint, roughly chopped just before serving

1 big cup cucumber, peeled and sliced thinly (a little thicker than the fennel)

1 big cup fennel, shaved/cut very thinly on a mandolin or with your sharpest knife – it's the thinness of the cut that determines how good the salad is

INDONESIAN **CHICKEN ON THE COALS**

How I love and adore this. The sauce is an addictive, deeply delicious concoction: hot, sour, savoury and very slightly sweet – just fantastic. It can be done in the oven instead of over coals, but the flavours beg for the smoky, charred caramel tones that only a fire can provide.

Be careful, if using breast meat, that you watch it like a hawk, and cook it only until just done in the middle. It develops the old-takkie syndrome so quickly.

This makes the perfect lunch served with steamed rice and Asian-style cucumber salad (see page 54), or with flatbread and a leaf salad. For some reason, these particular flavours pave the way for the most fantastic chicken–mayonnaise sandwiches the next day, so err on the side of bountiful.

The pre-fire preparation will take about 35 minutes, so prepare the fire accordingly.

In a processor, pulse the garlic and lemon grass until more finely chopped. Add the spring onion, terasi if using, chilli, dry spices, sugar and salt, and process until you have a coarse paste.

Heat half the oil in a large heavy-based pan, and stir-fry the spice paste for a minute or so. Add the chicken pieces, pour over the coconut milk, cover the pan and simmer on low. For thighs and drumsticks, cook for about 15 minutes, for breasts, only five minutes (so if using a mix, add these last).

Turn off the heat and leave the chicken to bask in the sauce for about 10 minutes.

Remove the chicken from the sauce, brush all over with the remaining oil and put on the coals. Cook on medium-heat coals until well browned on both sides – breast always takes much less time than leg meat, so place these more towards the centre of the fire, and the thighs and drumsticks over slower coals at the edge. You can put the breasts on when the drumsticks are half done, so that everything is ready at the same time.

While someone else is tending to the chicken, continue to cook the sauce, uncovered, over a medium heat until it starts to thicken. Serve alongside the chicken.

SERVES FOUR

4 garlic cloves, chopped

2 stalks lemon grass, chopped

1 bunch young, thin spring onions (or about 5 'normal' spring onions), chopped

½ teaspoon terasi (Indonesian shrimp paste, which I usually replace with Thai fish sauce)

½ teaspoon chopped red chilli

½ teaspoon turmeric

2 teaspoons ground coriander

1 teaspoon brown sugar

Salt (start with about 1 teaspoon, adding more if necessary later)

4 tablespoons vegetable or coconut oil

8 chicken breasts and/or chicken drumsticks (the drumsticks slashed through in many places to make for faster cooking).

400 ml coconut milk

LEMON-SOY-CHILLI PRAWN PARCELS ON
CELLOPHANE NOODLES

This is a slight adaptation of one of Braam Kruger's Kitchenboy restaurant dishes. The original recipe features coloured cellophane paper and a microwave and is called Cellophane-Cellophane, (admittedly a catchier title), but I cook them in baking paper in the oven. This version has vegetables and prawns (or cashews for a vegetarian version) steamed in a hot, lemony, garlicky soy sauce, all poured onto deep-fried bean-thread noodles. I find it addictive.

With all the issues around both farmed and wild prawns – massive coastal degradation, antibiotic use and the huge bycatch being the main worries – it's difficult to make a green meal from a prawn. Really, you shouldn't think of cooking this without first hunting down sustainably farmed or caught critters. There are a few supermarkets and fishmongers that stock Marine Stewardship-endorsed prawns, or prawns that are otherwise endorsed by independent groups. Happily, these also tend to be the best-quality prawns. They aren't cheap, but you only need three per parcel, and anyway, you shouldn't be stuffing yourself with them.

Preheat the oven to 200 °C.

Pile the vegetables, topped with the prawns in the centre of the paper. Mix all the sauce ingredients and pour over the lot. Tie the parcel with string or secure with toothpicks, leaving some air space inside. Place in the oven for around 15 minutes.

While the parcel is cooking, heat the oil in a medium pot. Test a strand of noodle – it should puff up almost instantly if the oil is ready. Deep-fry the noodles – not too many in the oil at a time, as they puff up hugely – making sure everything gets oiled and puffed equally. Drain on a paper towel.

Place the froth of noodles on a big plate, settle the parcel on top (with added ribbon if you feel it becoming), and serve. Chopsticks are the best utensils to use here. Tell everyone to open the parcel and turf everything onto the noodles. Some noodles will go soggy, others stay crispy. This is how it's meant to be. Eat immediately.

EACH PARCEL SERVES ONE

Big handful julienned vegetables – I like red pepper, snap peas, onion and carrot

1 tablespoon slivered spring onion

1 clove garlic, finely slivered

1 mild chilli, chopped and seeded

3 medium-to-large prawns, cleaned, in shells

Baking paper, about 40 cm square

Cotton (not synthetic) string or toothpicks

2 tablespoons fresh lemon juice (you could use lime juice instead)

1 tablespoon palm sugar or syrup (optional – I like the bit of sweetness with the chilli and citrus)

2 tablespoons good soy sauce

Oil for deep-frying

Small handful (when uncooked) bean-thread noodles

MIELIES EL LOCO

The original recipe for this comes from the great Gourmet magazine, and is apparently a very popular, authentic, trashy way of braaing mielies in Mexico. I've removed the ketchup and added garlic and coriander. Less loco, more flavour, I think. I know mayonnaise on a mielie does seem quite dodgy, but I promise you, these mielies are totally delicious, and so great-looking when done the apparently traditional way, with the leaves pulled back and tied up to make handles to minimise heat and grease on the hands of eaters.

Boil or steam the mielies for five minutes maximum, to soften the leaves. Let them cool, then pull the leaves back gently. Remove one loose leaf, and tie the others together with this leaf.

Mix together the mayonnaise, coriander, salty garlic and chilli, and spread all over the mielies.

Braai, turning regularly, until the mielies are browned, with the leaves on the coolest part of the braai.

Serve hot, adding some extra flake salt just before eating.

SERVES FOUR

4 yellow mielies

4 dessertspoons good mayonnaise (i.e. not too acidic, and not the kind with water listed as the main/first ingredient, which food technology has made possible. You need the oil in the mayonnaise.)

4 dessertspoons chopped coriander

1 garlic clove, mashed with ½ teaspoon salt

½ teaspoon mild chilli, chopped

BEST-EVER **PEANUT-HOISIN SAUCE**

The peanut sauces I'd met since my introduction to them in the early nineties all featured coconut milk somewhere. Then I came across this version, in which peanut butter and hoisin are the two stars, and was blown away. This is brilliant added to a noodle stir-fry, or with braaied chicken, spring rolls or fresh Vietnamese rice wrappers.

Heat the oil in a small pan. Add the garlic and chilli, and fry for a few minutes.

Whisk in all the other ingredients and cook a few more minutes. Leave to cool. Once cool, and the flavours have settled, check whether the salt, chilli and vinegar amounts are to your liking.

Depending on the type of peanut butter you use, the sauce might be too thick on cooling. In this case, just mix in a little water.

This sauce keeps in a bottle in the fridge for a good few weeks.

SERVES FOUR

2 tablespoons vegetable oil

1 clove garlic, finely slivered

½ red chilli, finely sliced, most seeds removed

2 tablespoons peanut butter, unsweetened

3 tablespoons hoisin sauce

1 tablespoon Chinese chilli sauce

2 tablespoons brown sugar

½ cup water

1 tablespoon rice vinegar

DUKKAH

Despite our love affair with Middle Eastern foods, dukkah, that fragrant wonder of crushed nuts, seeds and spices, is underused. When it's made with the freshest nuts and spices, and stored airtight – or, even better, eaten immediately – the results are sublime.

For an addictive pre-lunch snack, serve dukkah and the best olive oil side by side in small bowls. Dip torn up bread into the oil, then into the dukkah. Apply to mouth. Also monumentally magnificent is a fat spoon of full-cream yoghurt topped with generous dukkah, served over roasted brinjal. Grilled fish and chicken love a sprinkling of dukkah over them too, even more so if you have a lemon wedge and some chilli lurking nearby.

Toast the nuts in a dry pan, keeping a beady eye on them all the while – they tend to burn the second you turn your back.

Crush in a pestle and mortar or processor till finely chopped, but don't let them become a paste.

Toast the seeds and spices together, then process or smash until very fine. Mix in the salt and check taste.

Keep in an airtight, dry container (but not in the fridge) to stop the nuts and spices losing their mojo.

MAKES ONE JAR OF DUKKAH

½ cup best macadamia nuts or skinned hazelnuts, or a mix of both

¼ cup good pine nuts

¼ cup white sesame seeds

2 tablespoons coriander seeds

2 tablespoons cumin seeds

½ teaspoon black pepper

1 teaspoon flaked sea salt (or to taste)

LAMPEDUSA PIE

TOASTED NOODLE BUNDLES (WITH JUST ABOUT ANYTHING)

I just don't like the fettuccine family of pasta. They don't have the wonderful snap-bite of al dente spaghettini, don't have the sauce-grabbing charms of penne and other stubby, chunky shapes. But in this form, I love the stuff. The pasta is formed into little bundles, left to firm up, then given a surface browning so that when eating you have these fantastic mouthfuls that are part crispy, almost buttery, and part soft, into which the juices of whatever you're serving on top, have run. You can also use Chinese noodles, but they should be the broad, very firm, good ones.

What to top them with? I say anything, but that's not very helpful. Here are my favourite partners:

Fried duck breast, plus soy-sake broth skimming the ankles of the noodle bundle.

Slivered rump steak with piri piri sauce plonked all over the noodles.

Baby Roma tomatoes done hot in the pan with chilli, onion, herbs, coarse salt, olive oil, so that the tomato becomes a sort of sauce once punctured.

You get the idea.

And so to the pasta...

Cook the fettuccine as usual, and drain extra well, releasing all the steam too. Do not add oil.

While the pasta is cooking, oil about six ramekins (obviously, depending on your ramekin size, you might use more or fewer).

Pile the fettuccine into the ramekins, pressing down a bit. Once totally cool, cover each with clingwrap to keep the pasta flat, and chuck into the fridge to firm up. You're after the claggy stuck-togetherness that you're usually at pains to avoid with pasta.

A few hours later (or even 24), upturn the ramekins onto a wooden board to let the pasta bundles roam free, then heat the olive oil in a thick-bottomed pan and 'toast' the bundles on a medium heat until brown and crispy on both sides (careful when turning).

Depending on the brand, you may have a neat little bundle that adheres as if glued together, or something that starts to become a little undone. Both are fine.

You could go more rustic on the whole thing: if the ramekin moulding seems like hard work, instead spread the cooked pasta on a flat tray to firm up and get sticky, then cook it like a giant Afro hairstyle in a big pan or wok, turning as it browns.

Serve immediately with any of the ideas above or your favourite saucy stew. Creamy sauces aren't great with this pasta.

MAKES FOUR TO FIVE BUNDLES

250 g packet fettuccine (or broad Chinese wheat noodles)

A little vegetable oil for greasing ramekins

6 ramekins – the sort you use for crème brûlée or similar (They should be flat-bottomed containers.)

1 tablespoon olive oil

TSOONT VAANGAN (SOUTH INDIAN APPLE & BRINJAL CURRY)

Apple and brinjal (aubergine) are the happiest of companions, and a very traditional combination in many cuisines (try the apple & aubergine tarte tatin on page 28 too). This is ridiculously quick and easy, best eaten with lots of basmati or some hot flatbread, plus a big dollop of yoghurt and chilli on top.

Mix the fennel, turmeric, chilli and mustard seeds with the water.

Heat the oil in a heavy-bottomed pot, and fry the apple, brinjal and onion separately, one after the other, in the oil, each until well browned. Set each aside in a bowl as you go.

Put everything, plus the spice-water concoction, back into the pot and mix it all up.

Turn the heat down and cook on low until the brinjal is soft. This takes about 15 minutes, but if you like the apple and brinjals mushier, keep going. Add salt to taste. Serve hot.

SERVES TWO TO THREE

1 teaspoon fennel seeds

½ teaspoon ground turmeric

½ teaspoon chopped chilli (or to taste)

1 teaspoon yellow mustard seeds

4 tablespoons water

½ cup vegetable oil

2 Granny Smith apples, peeled, cored and cut into 8 to 10 wedges

550 g brinjal, chopped into blocks about two fingers thick each way

½ white onion, cut into thin slices

Salt to taste

LAMPEDUSA PIE

ONION & ANCHOVY **TARTE TATIN**

Really, really much nicer than quiche. Eat it with a spoonful of thick cream or crème fraiche and a pile of bitter, vinegary leaves.

Heat the oven to 180 °C.

Melt the butter in a heavy, 25 cm ovenproof frying pan or pan-like container. Scatter sugar over the butter and remove from the heat.

Peel the onions and chop the tops and tails off. Cut each onion in half, to create two thick wheels. Arrange as many as possible on the butter layer, then cut the others in half or quarters to fit the gaps.

Pour over the stock or salted water and sprinkle with the vinegar. Scatter the anchovies and thyme over.

Place in the oven for about 45 minutes or until the onions are golden, buttery, caramelised coils, and most of the liquid has evaporated. Take out of the oven, cook on the stove top on a low heat until nearly all the remaining liquid goes (if there is any left), then cover with a circle of puff pastry and tuck it all around the onions along the edge of the pan.

Bake for another 20 minutes or until the pastry is golden. Place a plate over the pan and flip both over so that the tart lands onions-up on the plate. Do not fear the flip: any onion pieces that fall out or get stuck on the pan can easily be wodged back into position.

Cut into four slices and serve post-haste with the cream and chives dolloped on top, and black pepper for grinding.

SERVES FOUR

30 g unsalted butter

2 teaspoons castor sugar

4 to 5 onions, peeled

1 cup chicken stock (good-quality liquid type, store-bought if necessary) or salted water

2 teaspoons red or white wine vinegar

4 anchovy fillets, very finely chopped

1 teaspoon fresh thyme

½ roll butter puff pastry (or home-made if you are up to it)

To finish
Sour cream

Chives

Black pepper

SWEET CHILLI & GINGER **DIPPING SAUCE**

There are a thousand Asian sweet chilli sauces on the market, and these have their place. The problem is that their thickness always comes from the addition of cornflour or xanthan gum, instead of being achieved by the slow boiling down of the sauce to create a syrupy consistency. This slight jaminess is so much nicer than the viscous wobble of starch- or gum-thickened sauce. Sauces thickened with cornflour or flour can be very good indeed, unfashionable though they may be right now, but in the case of chilli sauce, it's always too much, verging on blobbiness.

This sauce will keep just about forever in a clean jar – no need to refrigerate – and is so pretty with all the ginger slivers floating about that you might want to make extra and keep some to give away as a present.

Heat all the ingredients except the salt on a low heat, in a thick-bottomed pot. Watch carefully to prevent over-boiling. When the sugar is totally dissolved, turn the heat up a little. Keep cooking for about 20 minutes until the sauce becomes lightly syrupy.

Remember that it will become thicker on cooling, so stop cooking when it's a bit runnier than you want it to be in its finished form.

Remove from the heat, leave to cool, and add salt to taste. Pour into a very clean container.

MAKES ONE SMALL JAR

½ cup rice vinegar or white grape vinegar

½ cup water or orange juice (orange juice is delicious but shortens shelf life)

½ cup white sugar or palm sugar

½ red Thai chilli, finely chopped (most seeds removed if you don't want too much heat)

1 dessertspoon fresh ginger, finely slivered

Salt to taste

MALAY LAMB KORMA (GULAI KAMBING)

Forget the rich, creamy north Indian kormas – this is nothing like them. All you need to know is that it's monumentally delicious. The recipe comes by way of Rick Stein's stupendous Asian cookbook, Far Eastern Odyssey *(one of the only recipe books I own from which I have cooked almost every single brilliant dish). I won't pretend this is minimal work, what with the making of curry pastes and such, but the results are more than worth it. It has both depth and sharp freshness; both treble and bass notes, and everything in between.*

Serve it with piles of steamed long-grain rice and cucumbers roughly chopped and tossed with a little rice vinegar. A bowl of chopped fresh chilli would not go amiss on the side.

Trim excess fat from the lamb and cut into 4 cm pieces.

Heat two tablespoons of the oil in a large heavy-bottomed pan or pot over a medium heat.

Add the curry paste (see page 124) and fry for two to three minutes until it smells fragrant and the spices start to split from the oil. Add the lamb and fry for two minutes. Be wary of the spices burning.

Add the water and a teaspoon of salt, and leave to simmer on a low heat for an hour, stirring from time to time.

Add the coconut milk, tomatoes, lemon grass and sugar, and simmer for around 30 minutes or until the lamb is tender (depending on the cut you use, this may take longer, in which case replace the lid).

To finish, heat the remaining oil in a frying pan over a medium heat. Add the garlic, and fry for a few seconds until golden, then add the cumin seeds, dried chillies and curry leaves (and the shallots if you are using them). Let it sizzle for a few minutes.

Tip the garlic and spice mix into the curry, and stir in.

SERVES SIX

1 kg boneless shoulder of lamb, or equivalent in stewing lamb, leg of lamb or loin

5 tablespoons vegetable oil

1 quantity Malay korma curry paste (see recipe on page 124)

500 ml water

1 teaspoon salt

125 ml coconut milk

2 firm, almost under-ripe tomatoes, cut into wedges

4 fat lemon-grass stalks, very finely chopped

2 teaspoons palm sugar (brown sugar works well as a replacement)

Salt to taste

To finish
15 g garlic, finely sliced

1 teaspoon cumin seeds

2 dried red Thai chillies, halved

Roughly 24 curry leaves

1 cup shallots, crisp fried (optional)

MALAY KORMA **CURRY PASTE**

Heat a heavy-based frying pan over a medium-low heat. Add the coconut and shake about for a few minutes until golden. Tip onto a plate to cool.

Add the coriander, cumin and fennel seeds, and shake about until they darken slightly and become aromatic.

Tip into a spice grinder, and add the remaining dry spices, chillies, nuts and toasted coconut, and grind into a coarse powder.

Tip this into a processor with the shallots, ginger, garlic and oil, and mix to a smoothish paste.

80 g fresh coconut, finely grated (I used good shredded coconut, and it was excellent)

1 tablespoon coriander seeds

2 teaspoons cumin seeds

2 teaspoons fennel seeds

3 cm cinnamon stick

¼ teaspoon cloves

¼ teaspoon cardamom seeds

½ teaspoon black peppercorns

1 teaspoon turmeric powder

½ teaspoon grated nutmeg

4 dried red chillies

8 macadamia nuts

300 g shallots or onion, finely chopped

25 g peeled ginger, roughly chopped

15 g garlic

2 tablespoons vegetable oil

FRIANDISE

The restaurants my parents went to when my brother and I were small – the night-time ones, anyway – seemed to me then, as they still do now, to be the most wonderful and super-glamorous places on earth. And not just the restaurants themselves, but everything that surrounded the outings. The seventies make up the large part of these memories – a time when Johannesburg's night life for many suburban whiteys was very much about a continental, often French, bistro-esque experience. Fine dining covered both continental and British fare. The Bougainvillea, the Balalaika, Chez Zimmerli, Ile de France and the great Three Ships were the main hang-outs. All are now long gone. Most went quickly, as has always been Johannesburg's way. The Three Ships was around until my thirties, and so has its own clear and real memories, but the remaining bunch have melded in my mind, becoming a confused mass of dark-red banquettes, outsized white napery, cigarette smoke, French onion soup and Trini Lopez tracks.

Watching our parents leave, elegant and fragrant, as we, in our pyjamas, scoffed macaroni tossed with butter and All Gold tomato sauce (don't knock it till you've tried it) was, for some reason, very soothing.

Best of all was what came back with them at the end of such an outing: the glamorous, the holy, friandise. For me, this embodied all the mystique and deliciousness of the imagined evening out. At the time, this was almost the default after-dinner item at any vaguely snazzy restaurant, served either with the bill or with coffee.

Now and then I'd be half awake when my parents got back. Through half-shut eyes I'd see my mother come in, take a crumpled tissue out of her glimmery bag, and set the booty, in its equally crumpled mini-cupcake paper, on the bedside table. It might be marzipan and a cherry somehow woven together with chocolate, or a strawberry or gooseberry, coated in a thin caramelised sugar layer, slightly shattered by the journey in the bag, slightly gooey from being made hours before. I knew it was meant for the morning, but the second my mother left the room, I shoved the thing in my mouth, ate it glumptiously and went back to sleep. The contrast between the fine crackle of the coating and the softness of the interior was the best thing about them. And yes, you're right, I did have cavities.

STRAWBERRY FRIANDISE

This is my favourite type of friandise, with, if not exactly a recipe, then a method and some tips. It's enough for four people. Each mouthful is so intense that you don't want to overdo it. I really think you can offer them as the dessert. Few people have a sweet enough tooth to manage a pudding and then these too. They should be made no more than 15 or so minutes before eating, for absolute crispness.

Use 16 smallish, unwashed strawberries (the big ones really aren't as good for this), with green hat still on. You only need 12, but this leaves room for an error or two and a tasting. They can be dipped into the caramel inferno by gripping the leaves (best but most terrifying method) or skewering first with small wooden skewers or toothpicks so that your fingers aren't a millimetre from the lava.

Oil a large piece of baking paper or have a silicone mat ready.

Skewer each strawberry at the leaf end (if using this method).

In a heavy-bottomed pan or pot melt the sugar with the water on a low heat, until the sugar has dissolved. Turn up the heat and boil until the sugar turns dark amber. Test a blob by placing it in cold water. It should harden immediately if ready. The caramel might look crystallised in places, but this should disappear once you give it a mix. If chronic crystallisation occurs, you'll need to trash the lot and start again.

Whip the vessel off the heat pronto, tilt it so the caramel pools at one side, and dip the fruit into the caramel, turning to coat evenly and entirely.

You need to work horribly quickly, there's no denying it, but at a push you can reheat the caramel gently (just enough to get it liquidy, not enough to further brown it).

These are at their very best served with whipped cream on the side. The play between the juiciness of the berry, the sweetness and crack of the caramel layer and the bland, velvety airiness of the cream is quite monumentally wonderful.

Avoid making these in very damp weather, unless eating mere seconds after completion: the caramel loses its brittleness quickly, and turns sticky and soggy. The sog factor is quite pleasant with marzipan or chocolate fillings but hell with fresh fruit.

16 small strawberries, with leaves

120 g sugar

4 tablespoons water

Wooden skewers or toothpicks

GIN & TONIC

The bar at the Rand Club, downtown in Fox Street, is apparently the longest bar in Africa. Whether it is or isn't, it's a damn fine bar. This is where you must drink your icy G & T while perusing the menu. The food – think of it as Brit boarding school chic or Randlord retro – is uneven, to say the least, but that doesn't matter. The powder-blue main dining room is the most beautiful dining room in the city, and a great place to lunch. I love to watch ancient three-piece-suited mining magnates with beards in the soup still looking slightly miffed at the sight of women in their club. Especially if those women are having a very good laughy time. Is it wrong to be fond of a place that for so long was a temple of all-round exclusion? Exclusion by race, by gender, by culture? I have no idea. I can't make sense of any of it. But there seems something good about taking ownership of the space in a big way, precisely because you couldn't before.

The rules for a good G & T are simple, but usually not adhered to. First, obviously, you'd think, use a top-quality gin. Pile the glass with lots of good-tasting ice (the top cube should be almost at the top of the glass). Mix chilled gin and chilled tonic in the ratio you like them. I like a double tot of gin, and the tonic to the top. Always add a thick slice of lemon. A dash of bitters for a pink G & T is nice too. I believe a G & T, with its dry, palate-cleansing quality, is much more than a cocktail: it's the best match for any meal eaten tapas-style – i.e. anything involving lots of plates at the same time. It is happily unaffected by having dozens of flavours thrown at it, while most wines find this very stressful and act up.

NEGRONI

*If one cocktail is **the** cocktail, the alpha cocktail, I suppose it's the gin Martini. But second place in my book goes to the under-served Negroni. Invented by Count Camillo Negroni back in 1919/20 (accounts differ) when he asked the bartender to swop the soda water in his long Americano to gin, it is a coolly elegant aperitif, much more drinkable than the saccharine offerings that now crowd cocktail menus. It's red, classy, beautiful, and the exact opposite of the insanely sweet Cosmopolitan – also red, also beautiful, but not so classy – a ridiculous cocktail, and much too girly for anyone but Barbie. Even Ken would rather have a Negroni, surely.*

For each drink combine 1 tot (30 ml) Campari, 1 tot (30 ml) semi-sweet red vermouth (e.g. Martini Rosso) and 1 tot of the best gin in an old-fashioned glass or whisky tumbler-type glass. Fill with ice cubes and add a twist of orange rind (or wedge of orange – untraditional but more orangey).

Not everyone, especially outside Italy, is a fan of the extreme bitterness of Campari. You can make a very pleasant, and less bitter, drink – though snooty bartenders might snort with derision if you ask for it this way – with only half the amount of Campari, and more ice to dilute.

CAMPARI FLOAT

Even for people whose faces crinkle up at the mention of Campari, who just can't cope with the bitterness – and it's understandable – this is an approachable Campari option. I guess you would serve this as an after-meal thing – a pudding really, rather than a cocktail. It would be brilliant as the end to a hot-weather lunch or dinner where a solid sweet course seems unnecessary, perhaps if the meal has been very heavy or filling. It's barely a recipe, more an idea and it's not like it can 'go wrong', so check out the guideline and then play around as you wish.

Pour in the Campari, then the soda or lemonade. Carefully place ice cream on top seconds before serving. In fact, it may be best to put all the ingredients out and let everyone assemble their own floats, so they're at the ready to lap up the foaming mass that rears up after a few seconds. I suppose drinking this outdoors might be advisable.

PER DRINK

Old-fashioned glass or medium-sized tumbler (you don't want the drink too big)

1 tot Campari

Soda water or lemonade to about halfway up the glass (depending on how bitter or sweet you want it)

Huge scoop vanilla ice cream

BUTTERED HONEY FIGS IN THE PAN

When figs are at their best, it seems criminal to do anything much at all to them; all you need is a dollop of some great blue cheese. But if you can bear to cook them, this is about as good as it gets: so blitz-quick and simple, it's barely a recipe. Serve this with yoghurt for breakfast, or with mascarpone or ice cream as pudding.

Melt the butter in a thick-bottomed pan, then throw in the halved figs. Add all the other ingredients a few seconds later, except the yoghurt.

Let the figs bubble in the buttery sauce until just soft but still holding their shape (an optional dash of whisky at the end is great). Slip out of the pan into shallow bowls and consume immediately, with the yoghurt, mascarpone or ice cream (or even as is).

SERVES TWO

2 heaped tablespoons butter

4 to 6 figs, depending on their size, halved

1 to 2 tablespoons honey, depending on your tooth

Shake of cinnamon

Squeeze of orange juice

A few dollops of full cream Greek or Bulgarian yoghurt, for serving

BEST POSH **CHOCOLATE CAKE**

I've tried more recipes for this sort of chocolate cake – you know, the squidgy, low-profile, too-grown-up-for-icing type – than I can count, but this one is by far the best of its kind. It's moussey in the centre, crusty on the outside and not too sweet. Though it's not flourless, as many of its chic kin are, it certainly feels that way in the mouth.

Preheat the oven to 180 °C.

In a thick-bottomed pot or pan, melt the chocolate, butter and coffee on the lowest heat. Stir from time to time to help everything to melt evenly, and whip off the heat the second all the chocolate has melted.

Beat the egg yolks well and stir into the chocolate once slightly cooled.

In a large bowl, beat the egg whites until stiff using an electric mixer or hand whisk. Fold in the sugar tablespoon by tablespoon, so that each addition can dissolve properly before the next.

Have flour, cocoa and a sieve at the ready.

Fold the chocolate mixture gently into the egg whites, then sift in the flour and cocoa, and fold again until the mixture is almost uniform. The flour should be evenly distributed, but a few egg-white streaks are nothing to panic about, and are better left, rather than working the mixture to an airless death.

Pour into the prepared tin and bake for around 20 minutes. You want the centre damp and the edges already cake-like. Leave to cool in the tin before turning out.

Note: this cake is monumentally great as a pudding. If you go this route, bake it in a pudding-type dish instead, leave to rest for five minutes to settle, and serve while still hot with pouring cream or ice cream.

280 g best dark-chocolate buttons, or dark chocolate chopped up

140 g butter

About 45 ml very strong filter coffee or espresso

5 free-range eggs, separated

200 g castor sugar

90 g self-raising flour

2 tablespoons cocoa powder

23 cm spring-form cake tin, the base lined with baking paper

VIENNESE **CARROT TORTE**

I'd always thought of carrot cake as an American invention (well, after the years when I thought it was invented by the moms who ran the school tuck shop), but then I discovered this recipe in an ancient book of my mother's, The Viennese Cookbook. And why be surprised? The Viennese are the gods of cake making, and can conjure a cake from pretty much anything. Since the carrot cake took over the home baking industry and school functions world in the eighties, I didn't think I'd see a recipe that could make this cake credible and interesting for me again, but this, truly, is it.

I have used the word 'torte' (rather than 'cake') not to be swanky, but because that is what the book calls it, that is what the Austrians would call it, and because torte seems to denote something just a little more unctuous than 'cakey' cake, which this is. It's made with ground almonds rather than flour, which makes it more nutritious, more delicious and, yes, I'm sorry, more expensive. Another change is that the eggs are separated and the whites beaten. Lastly, the carrots can be cooked beforehand and puréed, rather than added grated, which, for some reason, I find most beguiling. All of this gives a very different mouth-feel to the carrot cakes we've had thrown at us over the last few decades.

Preheat the oven to 180 °C.

Line the bottom of a 24 cm-diameter spring-form cake tin with baking paper, and butter the sides well. It must be a spring-form tin, as the cake is light and easily broken. Do not follow my foolish whim (pictured), which involved me being seduced by the pretty shape of a petalled bundt tin, and then having to remove the cake in slices.

Mix the grated or puréed carrots with the almonds. Beat the yolks and sugar together until light and creamy, then add the carrot–almond mixture.

Add everything else, the cornstarch at the end. Mix together gently until well combined.

Beat the egg whites until just firm, but not till they become dry (they should hold their shape, but have soft rather than well-differentiated peaks). Adding a pinch of cream of tartar to the eggs will help to give you puffy whites speedily, but make sure it's only a pinch.

Fold the whites into the mix gently but thoroughly, then pile all into the tin, level the top and bake for around 45 minutes. Start testing after 40 minutes: as soon as a skewer comes out relatively clean, or with the bits that cling to it looking crumby rather than smeary, whip it out.

Leave to cool before carefully loosening the sides, and move the torte to a plate. Once totally cool, with not a murmur of warmth left, add the topping. This is just one cup of cream, whipped and sweetened with a tablespoon or so of castor sugar, and sharpened with orange zest. The pectin in the zest will help to 'set' the cream, keeping it firm for many days.

Base

500 g carrots, either pre-cooked and puréed, or very finely grated

500 g fine-ground almonds

8 medium eggs, separated

2 cups castor sugar

Grated rind and juice of 1 medium lemon

1 tablespoon rum (optional, I don't use it)

2 tablespoons cornstarch/ Maizena

Topping

1 cup cream

1 tablespoon castor sugar

Zest of 1 orange

THE BEST **DARK-CHOCOLATE BROWNIES**

Also, the quickest. Why? Because you make everything in one pot. Just melt the butter, bung the rest in, and stir like the devil. It takes minutes to put together. But that's not what makes these the best brownies – the one-pot thing is just a bonus. Their top ranking comes from the smooth creamy texture and intense chocolateyness. They verge on a set mousse, which is just the way I like brownies to be. Nothing is worse than a cakey brownie. This recipe is slightly adapted from one by brilliant American pastry chef Alice Medrich. I have downed the sugar though – French baked goods are marked by abundant butter, German by abundant eggs and American, it seems to me, by more sugar than I'd choose. I've also used salted nuts in place of regular, and omitted the salt in the mix. I like the contrast between the unsalted mix and the salty nuggets.

Preheat the oven to 200 °C.

Melt the butter in a thick-bottomed pan. As soon as it has melted, add the chocolate, swirl about, put the lid on and remove from the heat. Leave for about five minutes, then stir the chocolate and butter together.

Add the sugar, vanilla and eggs, one by one, mixing in well, then add the flour. Don't add the nuts yet though.

Mix all vigorously. Every other source I have for brownies insists they should be mixed very lightly, but Alice taught me that this is all wrong. Vigorous mixing with a big wooden spoon until the batter starts to come away from the pot sides makes for the most sublimely textured brownies. What improves them even more is to leave the batter to rest for anything from 30 minutes to 12 hours, just as you would with pastry (and this goes for biscuits, and anything containing non-self-raising wheat flour). I rarely have time for this waiting step though, and they're very good without the resting, but try it if you have the time. So mix until your arm aches, and then fold in the nuts.

Pour into a 24 × 24 cm brownie tin (that's a regular brownie tin). The dimensions are important: a bigger or smaller tin means longer or shorter cooking times. Bake for 15 to 20 minutes. They will seem far too liquid, but will settle once cool. Leave till totally cooled down before cutting or moving.

Actually though, you can also eat them hot, as a ganachey sort of pudding, which is arrestingly wonderful, but dastardly rich. Scoop the oozing batter out with a spoon while still warm, and serve in bowls. Eat this with ice cream or cold pouring cream and grate orange zest over everything.

Whether eaten hot or cold, the way to make these taste best is to serve small portions.

8 tablespoons unsalted butter

120 g best dark unsweetened chocolate – 70 to 80 per cent cocoa solids, chopped up, or buttons (if the percentage is lower, and/or the chocolate is sweetened, use only ¾ cup sugar)

250 ml castor sugar (1 cup)

1 teaspoon vanilla extract

3 large eggs

125 ml cake flour (½ cup)

100 g chopped salted mixed nuts – anything except peanuts

WHITE CHOCOLATE, CARDAMOM & PECAN NUT **BROWNIES**

If you like fudgy, vanillary flavours, and prefer dense, damp items to fluffy confections, these will be heaven for you. What you also need though, is a considerably sweet tooth. White chocolate is, after all, not really chocolate – it's more like baby formula in slab form – and so there's none of the bitter intensity that dark chocolate or cocoa would add to the mix. But oh, they are wonderful.

These brownies are brilliant with whipped cream that's had some orange rind stirred into it, or with not-too-sweet ice cream, or even crème fraiche. Eat more than one and you will need a lie-down afterwards, but that is surely a small price to pay.

Preheat the oven to 170 °C.

Melt the butter on the lowest heat imaginable, then add the chocolate and let that melt too.

Remove from the heat and mix the butter and chocolate together.

In a large bowl, beat the eggs, salt, sugar and vanilla until thick and creamy.

Beat in the chocolate mixture, then add the flour, nuts and cardamom, folding in very gently.

Pour into a 25 × 20 cm brownie tin (buttered or lined with baking paper).

Bake for about 25 minutes – they should be set on top and around the edges, and still totally gooey in the middle. When still hot, this will almost resemble raw batter when a tester is put into the centre. If they're starting to feel cooked inside before that time, whip them out of the oven. Leave until cool before cutting up.

These are also extremely good with a shot of double-strength espresso in the mix; just cook them for five minutes longer.

125 g unsalted butter

250 g good white chocolate, cut into chunks

4 large eggs

5 ml salt

300 g castor sugar

10 ml vanilla extract, real if possible

300 g cake flour

300 g coarsely chopped pecan nuts or Brazil nuts (or roasted, salted macadamias)

Seeds of 1 cardamom pod, finely crushed

PEANUT-BUTTER PIE

There is something plainly trailer-park trash about this recipe – the combination of peanut butter, cream cheese, biscuit crust and chocolate being quite bizarrely inelegant. And, of course, as is so often the way with such vulgar partnering, it's delicious. Addictively so. Also sickening, if you go beyond one slice.

This is an adaption of a recipe from probably the best local baking book around, Cakebread, Pudding and Pie, *by Callie Maritz and Mari-Louis Guy.*

Preheat the oven to 180 °C. Grease a 23 cm loose-bottomed tart tin, or a ceramic or glass pie dish. Bear in mind that the pie will be too squidgy to remove from the container, so choose the dish with that in mind.

Combine the butter and biscuit crumbs, and press firmly onto the base and sides of the tin. Bake for 10 minutes. There is something disturbingly wasteful, I know, about heating the oven for a 10-minute jaunt. You could try making the pie to end off a meal in which the main course is something roasted, and bake the crust before the savoury course goes into the oven.

Beat the cream cheese, sugar, peanut butter, butter and vanilla by hand if resilient, or with an electric mixer, until smooth and creamy. Gently fold in the beaten cream, adding it bit by bit initially.

Spoon the filling onto the cooled biscuit crust and smooth the top.

Heat the cream in a thick-bottomed pan. Add the coffee if using. Stir in the chocolate, turn off the heat and cover the pot. After about five minutes, the chocolate will be soft enough to mix in easily.

Pour the topping over the filling, and leave to set.

Unless the weather is really hot, this pie can be kept at room temperature for quite a few days.

Biscuit crust
125 g butter, melted

150 g biscuit crumbs – I like Digestives best

Filling
200 g cream cheese

180 g sugar

250 ml smooth unsweetened peanut butter

15 g butter, melted

1 teaspoon vanilla extract (or essence, sticking with the trash feel)

250 ml fresh cream, beaten to stiff-peak stage

Topping
125 ml cream (3 tablespoons less if using the coffee)

3 tablespoons hot brewed coffee (optional)

1 cup (150 g) dark-chocolate chips or chopped-up dark chocolate

PLAY WITH YOUR FOOD

Well, it should always feel like play, in an ideal gastronomic universe. But some stuff feels more that way than others – or maybe on some days everything feels less that way than others? At any rate, here are recipes that are either the sort of thing you usually buy already made – the falafel, the butter – so that making your own does feel as if you're playing a bit. There are also dishes that are a little trashy (cheat's ice cream) or a bit odd (spaghetti with Marmite). Of course, you should take the making of all of them terribly seriously.

BUTTER

How easy is it to make your own butter? Laughably. I love doing this with my children because it's quick, foolproof, and has that alchemical thrill aspect to it, which makes everyone feel incredibly clever. All you need is some good fresh cream – please, no long-life weird stuff here – and 10 minutes or so.

Use anything from 250 ml to 500 ml of cream the first time. Whip the cream using a stick, a KitchenAid, even a manual beater if you're feeling strong, but don't attempt it with a whisk – it can't cope with the thickness of the butter and will probably break. When we were little, my father showed us how to make butter just by shaking the cream in a jar, which is fun, but for this you need more time and stamina.

So, whip your cream. Continue well past the firm stage and into the worrying curdled-looking stage. Keep going, and soon a pale smooth mass will separate from the buttermilk (which you should keep to make pancakes the next morning).

Take the butter blob out of the bowl and knead it for a while to remove excess buttermilk. Unless you're going to get complicated with presses and such, note that home-made butter will be softer than the shop sort, as it's hard to remove as much liquid. Don't use it for frying, as it will spit.

... AND BREAD

While we're on the subject of butter, a few words about an excellent and slightly overlooked bread. The loaf in question is called Bolo de Caco, and is virtually the national bread of Madeira. It's also the bread of choice for the areas in Johannesburg where mainland Portuguese, Madeiran, Mozambican and Angolan communities are gathered, or have left their stamp. Once you try it, you're hooked.

It's a bap-like white bread with a charred crust, either baked on clay, stone or brick, or in a pot, with sweet potato giving it a particular velvety softness quite unlike any other loaf I know. It looks a bit like a giant English muffin and should be eaten on the day of baking. Whatever's left on the following day will lay foundations for the best version of garlic bread imaginable. And it makes the most perfect toast.

Happily, I see Bolo de Caco (which translates to something like shard or stone cake) making increasing inroads into areas far from the Lusitanian bits of town. If you can't find it, take a trip to the grocers and fishmongers in the city's southern and south-eastern suburbs to seek it out. You'll thank me, I promise.

PANEER CHEESE

Want something to replace chicken in the great north Indian curry sauces, which you can make in your sleep? Let me tell you that making your own fresh curd cheese – similar to ricotta, but firmer and less salty – is wonderfully simple. It also makes you feel very clever. I love making this with my children, who never cease to be gobsmacked by the fact that they can conjure a block of (admittedly, rudimentary) cheese from boiled milk and lemon juice. And actually it impresses me every time too. Cut it into cubes and serve it bobbing about in a saucy curry, or buttered, spiced, skewered and roasted.

Bring the milk to the boil in a pot big enough to allow for some bubbling-up activity, hovering over it like a hawk. If using the saffron, add it to the milk from the beginning.

As the milk comes to the boil, immediately add the lemon juice and remove the pot from the heat. Stir.

The curds and whey will magically separate in moments. But if the milk doesn't seem to have separated quite clearly after a few minutes, add more lemon juice and keep stirring gently.

Pour the steaming curds and whey into a clean kitchen cloth placed over a sieve atop a large bowl. Keep the whey – it's nutritious, has a mild, sweet taste and can be added to curries, lentil soups and so on, instead of water.

Twist the cloth closed, squeezing out most of the liquid. Leave the curds to drain in the cloth for an hour or so. If a mega-firm paneer is required, place a heavy weight on top, such as a tin of beans or a brick. Allowing more time will also help. I prefer the paneer quite soft though – just able to hold its shape, but not hard – so I don't use a weight.

When firm enough to hold its shape, cut the cheese into bite-size blocks.

Creamy, mild north Indian sauces, from korma to palak, are paneer's best friends. You can either brown the pieces a little first in vegetable oil, or add them straight to the curry.

Paneer will keep in the fridge – in its whey – for about a week.

MAKES 1½ CUPS OF CHEESE (SERVES FOUR WHEN USED IN A CURRY)

10 cups full-cream milk (must be full cream – no terrible skim milk allowed)

A few saffron threads (optional)

5 to 6 tablespoons lemon juice

LAMPEDUSA PIE

GREEN PEA **FALAFEL**

Not the sort of thing you imagine yourself making at home perhaps, but falafel are so, so much better that way. And what's more, they're hilariously easy. Soaking the chickpeas is the only thing that takes time, and it's not actually your time that's taken because you just plonk them in water to soak for eight hours or so while you carry on as usual. This version, a sort of Israeli falafel, includes green peas (and should really be called temayas).

Serve them with plain or gussied-up yoghurt (chopped coriander, chilli and lemon rind work wonders) and a salad. Hummus, of course, and guacamole, work well too. Pita, or another type of flatbread, is also good with these falafels, but not essential.

Blanch the peas in boiling water for one minute, then drain well.

Drain the chickpeas and blend in a processor with all the remaining ingredients bar the oil. Blend until the mixture is quite smooth (a few chunky bits are fine, but if the mix is generally chunky, it won't hold together).

Season to taste, erring ever so slightly on the side of over- rather than under-salting (deep-fried things like salt – think of chips).

Roll the mixture into litchi-sized balls, flatten them slightly into fat patties, place them on a greased tray and refrigerate for roughly an hour (a much longer fridge visit won't hurt at all though).

When the time to eat them arrives, heat the oil in a frying pan or pot or deep-fryer (at 150 °C) until a pattie dipped into the oil develops a lively but not rabid ring of oil bubbles around it. When the patties are browned all over, remove and drain. Eat while hottish.

SERVES EIGHT

1½ cups frozen peas (frozen are actually better than so-called fresh peas, which have usually been off the plant too long)

375 g dried chickpeas, soaked in cold water for 8 hours or overnight

2 small spring onions, finely chopped

1 clove garlic, finely crushed

1 teaspoon ground cumin

1 mild red chilli – optional

2 tablespoons freshly chopped mint

1 cup white breadcrumbs

1 egg

Sea salt to taste

2 tablespoons vegetable oil for pan-frying or enough to fill a pot or fryer if deep-frying

SPAGHETTI WITH MARMITE

The original recipe for this just plain charming dish comes from the equally charming Anna del Conte (the cook whom Nigella Lawson cites as the food writer who changed her life the most). I love how the recipe reflects her dual Italian–British experience. She recommends this as a great child pleaser, but I've tweaked it to include some finely chopped flat-leaf parsley, which has the effect of turning it into a surprisingly pleasing dish for grown-ups too. Of course, you could also sprinkle the parsley, as opposed to adding it to the sauce, so that parsley lovers and haters alike are happy.

Cook the spaghettini as you would normally (the thinner the pasta, the more important it is to leave it very al dente – it carries on cooking when you mix it with the sauce, and can go into overcooked mode in half a minute).

While the pasta is cooking, melt the butter and Marmite together in a small pot over a low heat. Drain the pasta, reserving some of the water. Add a few tablespoons of the pasta water and the parsley to the Marmite mix. Pour this little brew over the drained pasta, which you've put back in the pasta pot.

Add a little olive oil and more pasta water to slacken if the sauce seems too dry, then plate up and serve with more Parmesan than you initially think necessary.

MAKES FOUR SERVINGS

80 g dried spaghetti (I use spaghettini – it's just got a better mouth-feel)

50 g butter (approximately)

1 teaspoon Marmite

Pasta water

Four teaspoons finely chopped parsley (I think flat leaf is best here)

Olive oil

Freshly grated Parmesan and black pepper for serving

MARZIPAN

If I'd had any idea how ridiculously easy it is to make marzipan, I'd have done so my whole life. In fact it is actually simple enough for someone fairly fresh from the womb, say, a three- or four-year-old, to cobble together.

Most commercial marzipan is so overly sweet and so low in almond that it hardly offers a clue as to what real marzipan is about. According to the German Lübecker marzipan law (Lübeck being the city from which, arguably, the best marzipan in the world still hails), at least 75 per cent has to be ground almond, with no artificial flavourings thrown in. The premium range is around 85 per cent ground almond. By comparison, much of the stuff squatting on the average supermarket or even posh deli shelf is anything from 40 to zero per cent almond. Yes, you read correctly, zero per cent. The cunning makers of much industrial Christmas and wedding 'marzipan icing' long ago found a way of deflavouring peanuts (a dodgy enterprise in itself, surely), and adding pints of almond essence, and a truckload or two of sugar – and putting the word 'marzipan' on the packaging without being sued.

Given this dreadful scenario, I'm not surprised that there's a huge marzipan-hating contingent in the population. While it's true that marzipan, much like clogs and anchovies, is one of those things people either love or loathe, there are some haters out there whose bias has been formed by the not-marzipan that they've been exposed to. Lure them into nibbling on a golden nugget of your home-made version, and they'll be converted.

This recipe uses cardamom and orange, an old Middle Eastern marzipan tradition, but obviously you could also just make a straight one with these flavours left out.

The ratio of almond to sugar is a rough guide and can be experimented with quite a bit, with no fear of anything going wrong.

Mix all the ingredients together. The paste should seem too dry initially, crumbling and falling apart. Keep mixing, and knead with your hands if necessary to bring together smoothly.

Don't be tempted to add more liquid too soon. The mix will become smoother and wetter as you go. Only if you've been doing some sturdy mixing for many minutes and the crumbliness persists should you add more liquid – a few drops at a time. You want a super-firm paste, almost a stale play-dough consistency.

Shape now (see 'things to do with your marzipan' overleaf) or leave as a blob. If the latter, cover it tightly with clingfilm or wax paper, and store in an airtight container in the fridge, or at room temperature if it's not mid-summer. It keeps well for weeks, even a month or so.

The best marzipan has something of a ripeness to it, a perfumey resonance that comes from 'curing' it. I'm not sure what the exact process used by industry is, but leaving the stuff wrapped up in the fridge for a week or so before using it does seem to improve both flavour and texture. It's nice enough used straight after you've made it, but leave it to rest if you can.

MAKES ABOUT A CUP OF MARZIPAN

200 g finely ground blanched almonds (the more finely ground, the better)

100 g icing sugar

Water or strained orange juice – enough to make a stiff paste (start with about 15 ml, adding cautiously); I like orange juice best, but H_2O is standard

A little extra almond and sugar for adjustment

½ teaspoon ground cardamom

Rind of 1 orange, finely grated

THINGS TO DO WITH YOUR **MARZIPAN**

Obviously, you can eat it just as it is, cut into slices or blocks, or try it rolled in cocoa powder (if eating immediately), or dipped into melted black chocolate, leaving it to set for an hour or so. I confess that I have the slovenly habit of simply tearing off a hunk of the stuff from the mother-blob every time I pass the fridge. Those hunks, let me assure you, make a very passable breakfast alongside a cup of coffee.

This marzipan is also wonderful layered within the batter of any plain, nut-free, dark-chocolate brownie recipe.

Lastly, if you have a spare year or so on your hands, then try making nussipan, which involves hazelnuts instead of almonds (or half and half because most people find the all-hazelnut version too intense). The time factor is in getting the skin off the roasted hazelnuts. You might be lucky and know of a stash of already roasted and skinned hazelnuts in your vicinity, in which case this is obviously as quick as marzipan. It's also quite extraordinarily delicious.

CHOCOLATE GANACHE (FOR PROPER HOT CHOCOLATE, TRUFFLES AND GANACHE ICING)

Making ganache, a mix of best black chocolate and cream, takes hardly any time and still less effort. I think every home should harbour a pot of the stuff in the fridge. My favourite use for it is as hot chocolate: just dollop a dessertspoon of the stuff into a cup and serve steaming milk on the side. A shot of espresso in the bottom of the cup doesn't hurt either.

To use it as a topping for cakes, biscuits, profiteroles, and so on, just pour on while it's still warm.

To make excellent truffles, let it firm up in the fridge and then roll it into little balls, then roll these in cocoa. Truffles are best made in winter when they can be kept at a cool room temperature.

Heat the cream in a heavy-bottomed pot. When hot but not boiling, throw in the chocolate, stir to mix a little, put the lid on the pot and take off the heat.

After about 10 minutes, the chocolate should be totally melted, though it may not look that way until you start poking it about. Whisk the ganache mix until smooth and shiny.

If you're using it for hot chocolate, keep it in a Tupperware bowl or wide-necked jar in the fridge. When you need to reheat it be sure to do it on a very low heat.

MAKES ABOUT 300 ml GANACHE

250 ml single cream

210 g best bittersweet chocolate, either buttons (easiest) or chopped up (slight pain)

WHIP-UP & TRASH

At the heart of almost every food lover there lies a little (or sometimes more generous) patch reserved just for the foods that counter all epicurean leanings and certainly all nutritional sense. Cooks and eaters who pride themselves on their elevated tastes must at times, I have to believe, want to give their tongue, tummy and spirit a rest from complex and refined creations, and sink their teeth into something more wanting in subtlety: a voluptuous pink marshmallow maybe, or a packet of the oiliest chips with lashings of el cheapo vinegar. A chef friend of mine confessed to a hankering for those slimy little guava-hued tinned viennas, straight from the tin, with that primordial slick of brine still attached.

Though I'm generally an avid proponent of food that's unprocessed, not chemically anointed and so forth, I can't help feeling that a ban on all silly edibles is just wrong. The big thing is, don't for a single minute let yourself think of these things as food. Brief comfort and glee they may bring, but the healthy thing to do is to think of such snacks as edible toys.

Here is my favourite trashy indulgence, which has always gone by the name 'whip-up'.

This is simply jelly whipped up to a froth with Ideal evaporated milk. Most of you will know the sort of thing. But, as with everything edible, even trash can be badly or well made. With the right method and the right quantity of jelly to Ideal milk, this is heavenly; truly more than the sum of its modest parts. My grandmother invariably made it for us on our first day of summer holidays in Cape Town. We always got there just before lunch, and we'd run into the little dining room to check the sideboard. We knew that there would always be a quivering bowl of pastel puffery, usually pink (strawberry, apparently), every now and then green (laboratory lime flavour). I'm aware that nostalgia brings an added glow to all things, but, truly, it would take a real curmudgeon not to fall in love with this, just a little bit.

Make the jelly with the first half of the liquid the packet tells you about (the hot part and don't add the cold part). Leave the jelly to cool to room temperature. Do not cool in the fridge.

Once cool, put the Ideal milk and the jelly into an enormous bowl (the bowl of a Kenwood-like KitchenAid is big enough) and beat with an electric mixer until about four times in size, billowing, and almost as thick as whipped cream.

Pour into a serving dish and leave in the fridge for another hour or so (or up to a day). The dish must be completely sealed with clingfilm or similar so that fridge odours aren't absorbed.

Take out of the fridge about 10 minutes before eating, unless the weather is very hot.

While my fondness for this concoction stems from childhood eating, I think of it as fine grown-up fare too, in the right context: a silly party pudding, perhaps, or an appropriately unrefined end to a lunch of cottage pie and peas.

SERVES FOUR, PERHAPS

1 packet jelly (pink jelly is the obvious choice, but most other hues in the jelly pantone range work well too)

1 × 380 g tin Ideal milk, chilled 12 hours in the fridge, or 1 hour in the freezer (don't waste your time trying this with unchilled milk: it won't froth)

BRILLIANT CHEAT'S **NO-CHURN ICE CREAM**

Here is a recipe that's so trashy and such a cheat it's downright shameful. Of course, it's not actually ice cream – not technically – but more of a semifreddo. Never mind, it's cold and creamy, delicious and dead easy.

The ingredients (blush) are as follows: ½ a tin condensed milk and 500 ml whipping cream. Yes, good old condensed milk from distinctly industrially farmed cows. Believe me, I do laugh at myself for using organic cream to combat the situation.

Whip the cream until stiff. It must be really firm and hold small peaks, but be very careful not to go to the curdly-butter stage. Now fold in the condensed milk.

Scoop into a freezable container and freeze for about eight hours, after which time you will have a smooth, velvety mass. It's incredibly good sprinkled with chopped peanut brittle, or with bananas fried brown in butter, and/or with a large tot of whisky added to the mix just before freezing. I once mixed in a mug of pitted sour cherries before freezing, and that was pretty damn fantastic too.

CHOCOLATE SORBET

Nobody could read Jacob Kennedy's Bocca: Cookbook *and not fall quite a lot in love with the man. It's his enthusiasm (rather than the fact that he's owner–chef of the most lauded Italian restaurant in London) that makes you want to try every single recipe in his mighty tome, bar perhaps the 'Sanguinaccio', a chocolate pudding featuring copious lashings of pig's blood. This fantastic sorbet (100% swine free) is like chocolate ice cream magnified.*

Mix together the cocoa and sugar in a thick-bottomed pot. Add the water, slowly at first, stirring all the time to avoid lumps (the few you get will cook out, so don't stress too much). Add the glucose syrup or honey, and bring to the boil. Take off heat once bubbling, add chocolate and stir till melted and evenly mixed.

Cool to room or fridge temperature. Blend with a stick blender for extra smoothness. Freeze in an ice cream machine, as per machine's instructions.

Serve very small portions; it's very rich and almost a winter ice cream, if that makes sense.

SERVES FOUR

50 g cocoa powder, sieved

200 g castor sugar

500 ml water

50 g glucose syrup (available from chemists and health shops) or runny honey

250 g dark chocolate (around 70%), broken up or buttons

PEANUT-BUTTER & YOGHURT **CUPCAKES**

There's something about the addition of peanut butter that turns the usual spongy cupcake interior into a more velvety substance. It's a dense, rather than light, confection, but not at all stodgy. These beg to be very big cupcakes. I think that if you're in peanut-butter mode, you're also in stuff-your-face mode, and something small and dainty isn't going to cut it. I make them in large muffin containers, the ones with six to a tray, using giant cupcake papers (I am vehemently, even religiously, anti-muffin – the American ones – so only use them for these). If you want to or have to make standard-sized cupcakes, take the cooking time down to around 20 minutes.

Heat the oven to 180 °C. Cream the butter with the sugar, in a mixer or with a big wooden spoon. If it's winter and the butter isn't soft enough, cut it into cubes and soften it in the initial heat of the warming oven.

Add the vanilla, eggs and then half the flour. Mix in the peanut butter well, then the yoghurt and the remaining flour. You should have a soft consistency – a bit like very thick yoghurt – that falls from the spoon easily but is far from liquid.

Place the papers into the cupcake moulds and dollop in the mixture so that it comes less than halfway up the sides. Bake for about 25 minutes, or until just springy to the touch but not colouring up too much. Never over-bake – remember, they'll carry on baking once out of the oven. Leave to cool in the tray.

Icing

Mix all together until creamy and whippy, and apply thickly to the cupcakes. Depending on your peanut-butter brand, you might need to slacken the mix with a bit more butter, or add extra peanut butter if the flavour isn't strong enough.

Eat on the day, or at the latest on day two.

MAKES 9 OR 10 ENORMOUS CUPCAKES, 14 OR SO SMALLER ONES

170 g butter

¾ cup castor or light brown sugar

1 teaspoon vanilla extract

3 eggs

1¼ cups self-raising flour

2 heaped tablespoons smooth, unsweetened peanut butter

¾ cup normal low-fat yoghurt (i.e. not the type with added cream)

150 g butter at summer room temperature (In winter, slice butter and place in the oven while preheating for a minute or less. NB. It must not melt.)

150 g icing sugar

3 tablespoons peanut butter, preferably unsweetened

STRETCH & **EXPLORE**

No, this is not where I foist grimly challenging items on you – no pickled duck embryos, no brains, no fusion sushi (feta and strawberry makis are far more terrifying than any plate of offal) – or suggest insanely complex culinary acrobatics. In fact, not even a brioche features here. These are simply recipes and ideas that are about a slightly different way of doing something; that contain, from my perspective, some unusual ingredients, or just seem a bit off the beaten track. Some, such as the Lampedusa pie, are time-consuming; others are lightning quick to cobble together (the scorched asparagus, or the wonderful pata, which is more about a shopping spree than cooking).

MUSSELS WITH LIME-GINGER-CHILLI CREAM SAUCE

The mussels: The mussels served in most restaurants are the horrible, tough, granular half-shell frozen kind. And what's sad is that we now think that's how a mussel should be. Fresh mussels, when properly (and that means briefly) cooked, are truly silken, and taste of the sea in the best possible way. The frozen ones have no place in your kitchen or your mouth, so shun them. Ask a good fishmonger to source you the fresh ones; some of them will comply. Count on about 12 mussels per person. Scrub and wash the shells, pull the beard out (as much as possible), then plunge them into boiling water just until the nano-second they open, removing them individually as they do. You want them slightly undercooked.

It's an old wives' tale that the unopened ones should be discarded – well, certainly as far as farmed mussels are concerned. I've been eating and serving them for years. They are often the best and boldest, which is perhaps why they have the strongest closing mechanism. So fish these out just after all the opened ones are open and out. Slip a sharp knife between the shells, and cut through the small muscle that holds the shell together. You can prepare the mussels to this point a couple of hours ahead, and leave them covered in the fridge. When ready to eat, plonk them into the sauce below, and heat through just until hot, no longer.

The sauce: You can give Leah Tsonye a pint of water and a stone, and she'll make it taste delicious. Beautiful, ballsy Leah, our current head chef, started working for us in our first restaurant in 1999 in the scullery. When our erstwhile chef arrived blind drunk for the third time in a row on a busy Saturday night, he was fired on the spot, and I hauled Leah to the front of the kitchen to help me. In a few months, this amazing woman – who had never eaten, let alone cooked, any of the Asian, Middle Eastern or, for that matter, Eurocentric stuff we were doing – was playing with the ingredients with an ease and understanding that was almost eerie. She is a food savant, no exaggeration. This is really her sauce. The general concept was mine, lifted from an amalgamation of other sauces, but she brought it into being in a way that's better than I'd imagined.

Heat the oil and fry the garlic, chilli, lime or lemon rind and ginger for two minutes.

Add the wine and bring to the boil. Turn the heat to low and simmer for about 20 minutes, uncovered. Add the cream and water, and put on a low simmer for about 10 minutes. Add the turmeric, salt and sugar to balance, plus more chilli if necessary. The sauce should be very pungent, and intense in all directions: strongly spicy-hot, sharp, sweet (but not too sweet) and creamy. Adjust if necessary.

Add the baby tomatoes and cook for five minutes, then add the mussels to heat through again if already cooled. Pour into bowls, top with the spring-onion slivers and serve immediately with loads of steamed long-grain rice or crusty dipping bread.

This sauce is also very good, as you can guess, with white fish such as hake. Just cook the fillets in the sauce on a low simmer.

SAUCE FOR EIGHT GENEROUS PORTIONS

2 tablespoons vegetable oil

2 teaspoons slivered garlic

1 teaspoon chopped red chilli

1 teaspoon lime rind (or lemon if limes are not about)

2 tablespoons slivered ginger

400 ml white wine – something off-dry or sweet

1 litre cream

250 ml water

½ teaspoon turmeric

Salt and sugar to balance/taste

Spring onion, slivered, 1 tablespoon per serving

A handful of baby tomatoes for serving

THE MIGHTY **PATA**

The same plant that gives us the madumbe – that is, the taro, or elephant ear leaf plant* – also gives us, after a fair amount of hard labour on the cook's part, the wondrous pata. Pata is made from taro leaf and masala paste, rolled up Swiss-roll style. It's sliced and fried, usually served atop tiny puri breads and sold as 'puri pata'. It's considered a snack, a walking food, not even a sit-down starter, so you won't find it in many restaurants. It looks like nothing more than a burnt something or other but, oh my goodness, it tastes indescribably good.

From the first time I tasted a pata, bought from a minuscule Indian eatery, Anjan's, near Durban's Grey Street, I was instantly addicted. There's a bitter, burnt, herby thing going on that tastes like absolutely nothing else. I spent the following few weeks obsessed with it, and the next time I was in Durban, my drive from the airport was straight for the little puri pata den. It took a few months of questing before I managed to track pata down in some of Johannesburg's Indian delis.

Pata remains very much a Durban thing. Unlike almost all other Indian food, it is still only really popular in the Indian community. I'm always surprised that this delicious item is so little known. Maybe it has something to do with its unglamorous looks?

I'm not for a crazy moment suggesting you make your own from scratch, but I am definitely encouraging you to take a trip down to your local Indian deli and ask about buying pre-rolled, pre-sliced frozen pata.

Thaw the roll, and shallow-fry or bake it with generous amounts of a very neutral olive oil, or peanut or sunflower oil, on both sides. Be generous with the oil. Though traditionally served on top of Indian fried breads – little puris – pata is very good with a number of other things too. The cool balm of yoghurt is really what the pata wants, well perhaps to my comparatively namby-pamby un-Indian palate. So tzatziki, or Indian- and Pakistani-type yoghurt dips work brilliantly, as does a yoghurty guacamole, or a yoghurty hummus. Plus lemon wedges on the side. If puris are out of the question, Mexican-style flatbreads or freshest pita breads are a perfect alternative. You can eat pata hot or cold.

* A tiny warning: though this is very rare, some people are particularly sensitive to the oxalic acid in the taro leaf, which renders the leaves toxic when raw; and even once cooked, pata leaves can cause skin allergies and stomach aches.

SOMEWHAT ETHIOPIAN-STYLE **STEAK TARTARE**

I first met up with this recipe in Dorinda Hafner's book A Taste of Africa, and then in real life at the Abyssinia restaurant, in its first incarnation in 'Little Addis', downtown on Jeppe Street. Theirs was quite different from Ms Hafner's, and I've met other variations since then, so I don't feel that tweaking it a bit is altogether in the wrong spirit. I think my version – with the addition of sesame seeds and olive oil, and sans garlic – is pretty much unbeatable (though perhaps the Ethiopians would not agree).

If you're making this for people you suspect might be squeamish about raw meat, the best trick is to cut the meat paper thin, as per carpaccio, instead of mincing it, and use the condiments as a dressing drizzled over (as in the photograph). Have you noticed how the same people who get freaked out about eating raw meat when it's minced à la tartare will happily scoff plates of the stuff in the elegant Italianate-shavings format?

If going the mince route, I like serving this in the French tartare mode, i.e. with a small central mound of the mince circled by a throng of condiments. Again, this is hardly traditional, as the meat and spices would usually be pre-mixed, but I think people like the chance to make a bespoke meal for themselves, with each mouthful – if they wish – being different from the one before. Topside, sirloin or rump are best, with all tendon and outside fat removed (marbling fat you can certainly leave in though). Ask your butcher to mince it for you coarsely (if your visit is just prior to eating), or hand-chop it with cleavers, which gives the best result by far.

To make the dressing, mix the dressing spices, lemon, onion and olive oil, and season quite highly (raw meat likes quite a bit of salt).

Toast the sesame seeds in a dry pan, watching like a hawk, until golden.

Divide the meat into four, shape into rounds or sear and slice as in the image. Place each in the centre of a plate, in as attractive a little hemisphere as possible.

Surround each portion of meat with a lemon wedge, the sesame seeds, peppers, chilli and salt in little piles, and the dressing in a tot glass.

Traditionally, this would be eaten with that wonderful, huge, spongy, sour injera flatbread, made from teff grain. But warm pita, tortilla or hot wrap bread work well, and even sourdough is good.

Also customary, and I think essential, is to eat lots of raw chopped stuff with the meat. Ethiopians serve vegetables. My take on this is an assortment of leafy, herby things – undressed watercress, rocket and/or coriander are perfect.

SERVES FOUR

400 to 500 g top-quality (that means pasture-reared) lean beef, chopped.

Dressing

1 teaspoon ground cumin

½ teaspoon each ground cinnamon and coriander

Juice of 1 lemon

1 onion, very finely diced

4 tablespoons olive oil

Salt and freshly ground black pepper

Condiments per person

1 teaspoon white sesame seeds (the traditional recipe doesn't have these, but believe me, you want them)

Lemon wedge

1 tablespoon mixed red and yellow peppers, finely diced

½ teaspoon or so of chopped chilli

Small heap of extra salt – coarse-ground or Maldon

SCORCHED **ASPARAGUS**

My totally favourite way of eating asparagus. For the best charred, smoky flavour you need a hob with a flame big enough to creep into the wok or pan when you tilt it, to set fire to the oil. But it's still very nice without this happening – just use a high heat throughout to get the blackenedness, which is where the taste is.

Coat the asparagus in the oil.

Heat a dry pan or wok until scarily hot – far hotter than you think it should be.

Throw in the asparagus with any loose oil and toss, for about two minutes, or until they are tender but definitely not wilty and sad. Tilt the pan or wok away from you while cooking to get the oil to catch alight, if possible.

Tumble onto a plate and dress with the vinegar, then scatter the salt, sesame seeds and Parmesan shavings over the lot. Some bread on the side is a good notion.

FOR PERHAPS TWO

1 fat bundle thin green asparagus

2 tablespoons olive oil

Splash of red wine vinegar

Good flake salt, sea or other, to your liking

2 heaped teaspoons white sesame seeds, toasted (in a dry pan, watching like a hawk)

Handful of Parmesan shavings

HUMMUS BAKED WITH PINE NUTS & BUTTER

A fine curiosity from Anatolia, this hummus is served piping hot. Eat it with grilled meats, vegetables, boiled eggs, flat-bread, or – as I find myself doing – on a big fat tablespoon all on its own. Of course, you could also eat it cold.

Preheat oven to 180 °C.

In a processor, blend the chickpeas, olive oil, lemon juice, garlic and cumin until smooth. Stir in the tahini and yoghurt, and check seasoning. Pour the mixture into an ovenproof dish roughly 15 to 20 cm in diameter, and flatten the top.

Toast the pine nuts in a dry pan until browned. Add the butter and paprika, and heat till the butter is melted. Pour this mix evenly over the hummus.

Bake for 25 minutes and serve immediately.

MAKES ENOUGH FOR FOUR

3 cups cooked chickpeas (if using dried, soak 1 ½ cups overnight and boil for an hour)

¼ cup olive oil

Juice of 2 lemons

3 garlic cloves, crushed

2 teaspoons cumin seeds, crushed

3 tablespoons tahini

3 tablespoons thick, creamy yoghurt

Salt and black pepper to taste

3 tablespoons pine nuts

3 tablespoons butter

2 teaspoons good paprika

CAULIFLOWER CHEESE THE WAY IT SHOULD BE

I like the standard Sunday lunch-type cauliflower cheese, I do. But I think it could be infinitely more interesting. Here's a version that you could eat as a dish on its own, with maybe green leaves and bread lingering nearby. It's spiked heavily with capers, melty onion and, in the final best version (made after the pic was taken, I fear), copious parsley.

Heat the oven to 180 °C.

Melt the butter and oil in a thick-bottomed pan and fry the onion on the lowest heat until golden and soft.

Pour the cream into the pan with the garlic, Parmesan, parsley, anchovy and capers.

Add salt and pepper to taste.

Break the cauliflower up into smaller florets, or slice thickly. Put into an ovenproof dish – about 18 cm in diameter, then pour the cream mix over. Make sure the cauliflower is pretty much covered by the sauce.

Bake uncovered for about 40 minutes or until speckled golden-brown.

Serve alongside a roast chicken or with a vinegary salad and bread.

SERVES TWO

1 tablespoon butter

1 tablespoon olive oil

1 onion, finely sliced

1 cup cream

1 clove garlic, very finely sliced

2 tablespoons Parmesan, grated

1 tablespoon parsley

½ teaspoon anchovies, chopped

2 teaspoons capers, chopped

Black pepper and salt to taste

300 g cauliflower

HOME-CURED **DUCK BREAST**

If there's only one recipe you make from this book, please let this be it. It's yet another one that comes via my favourite cook, Braam Kruger. I haven't fed it to a person who didn't fall slaveringly in love with it. Don't bother to make this if you're not going to relish every bit of the heavenly fat. Cutting it off defeats the whole point of the recipe.

Lay the duck breasts in a non-reactive tray (i.e. ceramic or glass) and rub with the vinegar. Add everything else and mix up thoroughly.

Place the duck skin side up, making sure the salt is evenly distributed, and cover with a lid or clingwrap.

Leave in the fridge overnight or for about eight to ten hours.

Remove the duck from the spice mix, shake and wipe all the salt away by hand or with a clean cloth. Blot totally dry with more kitchen cloth or kitchen paper, pressing into the nooks and crannies. Drying the surface well is vital.

Put stainless-steel hooks or thread string through one end of each breast and hang them in an airy, dry inside space well away from sunlight. They shouldn't touch one another. The weather should be cold to temperate (even spring in Johannesburg is cool enough). After two days, your duck will feel dry and biltongy on the outside, but still rich and soft in the centre. Do not over-hang. Remove the hooks or string. You can keep the duck in the fridge for up to a few weeks, wrapped in wax paper or in a container, before you serve it.

Just before serving, heat a dry pan till blazing hot, and press the duck skin-side down onto the surface until the skin is very well browned. This should take seconds, and it's imperative not to let the flesh heat up. The skin browning-and-crisping step is not to be missed out: the contrast between semi-liquid fat, crisp skin and almost coppa-like meat is indescribably glorious.

Immediately after browning, slice very thinly, and eat pronto, either on its own (I highly recommend a few pieces in the mouth seconds after it comes from the pan), or on top of a green leaf salad, very scantily dressed. I think a slightly sweet vinaigrette flatters the duck best, and a scattering of toasted sesame seeds is almost compulsory.

FOR FOUR DUCK BREASTS

6 tablespoons balsamic vinegar

6 tablespoons coarse salt

1½ tablespoons crushed black peppercorns

1 teaspoon allspice (aka Jamaican pepper)

¼ teaspoon crushed cloves

2 tablespoons crushed coriander seeds

CRISP-FRIED FISH WITH PINEAPPLE, GRANADILLA & CHILLI SAUCE

Whole crisp fish with an almost plastic-shiny fruit-studded spicy syrup atop – it's like Chinese sweet-and-sour fish gone Bollywood. This is a slight adaption of a Braam Kruger (alias Kitchenboy) recipe. Braam knew fish. He knew how to catch them, how to store them, how to choose the best ones in a fishmonger and how to cook them (it was the only food area where he had green leanings, making sure that he never used threatened species). Sadly, there are only a handful of fishmongers in Johannesburg who know or care much about any of these things. Generally, fish is abused and disrespected, both in the sourcing and the cooking. And with so little fish bought from specialist sellers compared to the supermarket, it's hardly surprising.

Perhaps it's an inland problem. Perhaps we shouldn't be eating sea fish at all? But we do, and so we should do it right. This recipe calls for a whole fish (a lean, white-fleshed variety) and, of course, whole is really the best way of cooking fish. Under heat, the gelatine from the skin and bones runs into the flesh, making it velvety and unctuous, and the silken flesh in the head is there for the devouring. Also, if the fish is still on the bone, deep-frying it means you get a crispy tail and fins, which is the fish equivalent of crackling on the pork roast. And another merit of buying fish whole is that you can judge the freshness more easily: the eyes must be translucent and convex; the skin should spring back out when you press it; the gills should be bright pink or red rather than anything approaching brown (almost the easiest giveaway with old fish); and, perhaps obviously, the fish shouldn't smell. For that matter, neither should the fishmonger.

Put all the sauce ingredients into a pot with enough room for some bubbling up, and simmer away until reduced to a thin syrup. Keep it warmish, but there is no need for it to be boiling when you apply it to the fish. What is important is that the fish is still hot – this way, it seems to soak up some of the syrupy sauce, much as a hot koeksister does.

A wok is the best way to deep-fry a large fish – the contour holds the thick body of the fish; the head and tail peep out and get less oil, and cook more slowly. If you don't have one, ask the fishmonger to cut the fish into thick steaks so that you retain the benefits of the skin and bones.

You can also do this recipe with chunks of fish fillet, skin on or off. Essentially, this produces amped up sweet-and-sour fish nuggets. This way, you can deep-fry the fish in pretty much any container.

Slash the fish deeply, diagonally, on both sides. Apply salt to the fish and leave for 30 minutes. Wipe all the salt off (rinse it if you need to, then pat dry). Dredge the fish in the cornflour. To do this, put the cornflour into a plastic bag

Sauce

1 litre pineapple juice

1 cup cider (or rice) vinegar

1 cup sugar

1 tot dark rum

1 tablespoon slivered ginger

1½ cups granadilla pulp

2 Thai chillies, finely chopped

1 small pineapple, cut into wedges

2 sweet peppers, 1 red, 1 yellow, cut into thin strips

Salt to taste

(Continued overleaf)

(Crisp-fried fish continued)

with the fish and toss together, then remove excess cornflour; this makes the least mess and uses the least cornflour.

Deep-fry the fish, turning it over carefully when you judge it to be half done. When browned on both sides and the flesh is opaque and comes away from the bone at the thickest part, the fish is done. Don't fry it for a second longer. Lift it from the oil using a sturdy drainer/lifter, blot with kitchen paper, transfer to an enormous platter and while still hot, pour the syrupy sauce over it. Serve immediately, with plain steamed rice alongside – short grain or jasmine, never ever parboiled.

SERVES FOUR

The fish

1 large (about 1.5 kg) or 2 medium linefish, descaled only (fins and tail left on)

Handful coarse salt

Cornflour for dredging

Vegetable oil for deep-frying – enough to half fill a wok (in which the fish fits comfortably)

HOW TO COOK **FRESH PORCINIS**

By 'fresh', I mean to distinguish them from their dried brethren. I'm not referring to their freshness, as in plucked that day (though that too does count). I've come across many great recipes for these fleshy wonders, but there's one thing missing for me: I am adamant that the stems and caps should be cooked separately, or at the very least, staggered. If porcinis are cooked until the woodier stems are tender, the caps have become too mushy. Conversely, if you want the caps firm, then you end up with slightly woody stems. With the very smallest (i.e. the best) and most recently plucked specimens, the difference is minor, and you can happily throw everything on the heat together. But with the larger ones, and especially if they're not supremely fresh from the earth, it really makes a massive difference (the stems get woodier and the caps mushier every day).

Another mistake commonly made is not sautéing porcinis on a high enough heat, with the result that the umami aspect, which is brought out so well by caramelising the surfaces, isn't there. A boiled effect is not what you want. Try this method and I bet you'll never cook them differently again.

Heat the olive oil in a thick-bottomed pan, then add a single layer of porcini stems. Sauté both sides until brown, then add the caps and garlic, and continue frying until they're softening but still hold their shape. Add basil and salt to taste, and the lemon juice if you are using it. Add black pepper if you like.

To serve with pasta, dress cooked penne, macaroni or other stubby-shaped pasta with the smallest amount of olive oil then spoon the mushrooms on top. Alternatively serve on a pile of silky mash, on polenta or just on toast. They could also – in a possibly vulgar, but certainly delicious, move – top a fillet steak. In this case, skip the Parmesan.

FOR TWO

2 tablespoons olive oil

350 g porcinis, stems and caps separated, and both sliced

¼ to ½ teaspoon garlic, finely slivered

1 tablespoon basil leaves, torn up

Salt to taste

Lemon juice to taste (optional)

Black pepper (optional)

Parmesan for the table

LAMPEDUSA PIE

IVORIAN-STYLE **WHOLE FISH ON THE COALS**

Anna Trapido – without doubt the funniest, cleverest and most interesting food writer and broadcaster in the country – lives on a farm near Pretoria, but knows more about the African cuisine available in Johannesburg than most of the city's own residents. Through her, I came to know Etienne Gaba. Mr Gaba is a charming host and a brilliant chef. He runs a makeshift restaurant from his house in Yeoville, for a while now home from home to a tight-knit community of mainly West African immigrants. By day, regulars wander in and get served whatever deliciousness is in the pot; by night, the regulars are interspersed with other diners, mostly unversed in West African food, who book for Mr Gaba's fantastic banquet-style dinners, eaten in the cement courtyard out back under a huge palm, or in the bedroom-converted-to-dining room, inches from a wide-screen TV fixed full blast on MTV.

One of the most delicious things I ever tasted at the Ivorian was whole tilapia fish laid out on a big braai in the backyard and basted all the way through its coaly journey from raw to cooked with a mixture of grated root ginger, oil, lemon, salt and black pepper. The taste is deeply satisfying, and even more so if you serve it, as Mr Gaba does, with a tomato and chilli relish (what I would call a salsa in another context) and manioc (cassava tubers worked to a couscous-like crumble). I know you might happen to be out of your usual supply of manioc this week, but never fear – couscous will do very well in its place, as will long-grain steamed rice, which chef Gaba also sometimes uses. The tomato-chilli thing, though, is essential.

In place of tilapia, any whole white-fleshed fish (i.e. non-oily), will do, but please, I hardly need say, use something SASSI-approved.

For four people, use a whole fish weighing 1.2 to 1.5 kg, but the exact weight, within reason, is not critical. The basting amounts and cooking time below are for a 1.5 kg fish, so adjust the basting quantity and the time, as necessary. Ask the fishmonger to take the scales off but leave the fins and all else intact. Be clear about this: fishmongers love nothing more than to chop heads and fins off without a by your leave, and there's nothing better than the silken flesh in the head or the crispness of the cooked fins and tail. The fish must be impeccably fresh. That means the eyes will be bright, translucent and convex; the flesh springs back out when you press it; the gills are still red or pink, rather than brown; and, perhaps obviously, it shouldn't smell fishy at all.

Mix all the basting ingredients together in a bowl.

Slash the fish deeply on both sides, diagonally along the body, then sprinkle with salt on both sides, rubbing it into the slashes, and leave to drain in the sink or a large baking tray. Salting firms up the flesh, and while it's not essential, it greatly improves the eating. After 15 minutes, wash the salt off and press the fish dry thoroughly with a kitchen towel.

To braai, you need a fish grid, unless you're madly confident about turning a fish without breaking it. They

(Continued overleaf)

1 whole fish, about 1.2 to 1.5 kg

Kosher/coarse salt for salting fish – about 4 tablespoons

Basting
8 teaspoons freshly grated ginger root (grate very finely, discard very fibrous bits)

2 teaspoons sea salt, flaked or ground

2 teaspoons black pepper – ground just before using

Juice of 2 to 3 lemons, depending on size

6 dessertspoons vegetable oil or mildest olive oil (plus a bit more for initial greasing)

manage it at the Ivorian, by some miracle, but I try to avoid this. If you can't find the special fish-shaped ones, smaller fish will be fine in a normal old boerie grid.

Rub the fish all over with some oil, place it in the grid and lay it over the coals. From about five minutes, keep applying the baste, turning the fish maybe twice, and basting till it's done. I can't tell you exactly how long this will take – it depends on both the fish size and the fire. But the bigger the fish, the slower the fire should be. Count on about 15 minutes per side for a 1.5 kg fish, but the only real way to test whether it's cooked is to pull the flesh apart where it's thickest: the instant it's no longer translucent and can come away from the bone easily, whip it off the heat.

For the tomato sidekick: this is just tomatoes and onion chopped very small, heavily doused with chilli and, in my version, lots of coriander leaf. Very plain.

Extra oil and lemon on the side never hurt.

SERVE THREE TO FOUR

PERSIAN **MINTED ONION SOUP**

Sharp, fragrant and light, this brilliant soup – which I've adapted slightly from British chef Paul Gayler – can be made using vegetarian stock instead of chicken stock, if you prefer, but it needs to be really full bodied (and definitely not that bizarre powdered stuff).

Heat the oil in a heavy-based pot, and fry onions on low with the spices for a minute or so. Add the water and cook another 10 minutes on low, until liquid is gone and onions are golden.

Sprinkle flour over the mixture and cook for two minutes. Add stock gradually, stirring all the time.

Bring to the boil and leave to simmer for about 30 minutes, or until onions are totally soft. Add the lemon and lime juice, the sugar, and possibly salt, depending on your stock. Stir in the mint and serve.

SERVES FOUR TO FIVE

1 tablespoon olive oil

4 large onions, very thinly sliced

¼ teaspoon ground turmeric, or a few saffron strands

¼ teaspoon ground cinnamon

¼ teaspoon freshly ground cardamom

4 tablespoons water

1 tablespoon flour

1 litre chicken stock

4 tablespoons lemon juice (or to taste)

3 tablespoons lime juice (or to taste)

1 teaspoon castor sugar (or to taste)

2 tablespoons slivered mint leaves (or more)

TETSUYA WAKUDA'S **MISO & BLUE-CHEESE SAUCE** (FOR BRINJAL, LAMB, GRILLED CHICKEN AND MORE)

One of Sydney's greatest chefs, Tetsuya Wakuda is famous for creating great depth and complexity of flavour with the simplest methods and minimal ingredients. On the face of it, this sauce, from his wonderful cookbook, Tetsuya, smacks of the most desperate sort of fusion fare: who would ever think of coupling Japanese miso with any dairy at all, let alone smelly blue cheese? But once you try it, you realise both the logic and poetry in the combination. Both are aged products, with a strong umami factor, and they're total bliss together. I've made it slightly less chefy – no need to strain sauces through a sieve, I'm thinking – but essentially it's the same.

As the recipe title suggests, you should try this with many things (I've tried it as a snazzy partner to beef fillet, for example, and it's great). Just steer clear of seafood and all will be well.

Bring the stock to a simmer, then whisk in the miso and add the cheese, letting it melt in while stirring. Add the remaining sauce ingredients, checking the balance as you go (miso pastes differ widely in thickness and saltiness, so expect to do some adjusting). If the sauce seems too thin, let it simmer uncovered for a while.

Pour over, under, around, roasted brinjal, lamb, chicken – or whatever it's accompanying.

The sauce does cry out for some sharp greenness to counter its richness, so a scattering of finely sliced spring onions or some small, sharp, bitter herbs will be welcome.

SAUCE FOR FOUR PORTIONS

+/– 250 ml chicken or vegetable stock

100 g Japanese white miso paste (medium brown is also fine, but not the intense dark-brown one)

15 to 20 g best creamy blue cheese

1 teaspoon soy sauce (test before adding; the blue cheese may be salty enough)

1 to 2 teaspoons mirin

1 teaspoon ginger, very finely julienned

LITTLE COUGH QUAIL

At The Leopard we serve quail with macadamia stuffing, and the chilli fumes in the sauce always leave everyone under the extractor hood in our kitchen hacking, but in a restrained, staccato way so that customers don't feel invaded by the coughing attack. That explains the silly name.

Mix together the stuffing ingredients, up to a day ahead.

To make the sauce, fry the garlic in the oil until softening. Add the chilli, tomato and olives, and simmer for about 15 minutes. The sauce should be thicker than a napoletana, with the oil separating out a bit. Throw in the coriander; add salt and sugar. Check seasoning and take off the heat. This is something you can make beforehand – even days before – and reheat when ready to serve.

Preheat the oven to 200 °C.

Carefully push the stuffing into each quail's body cavity, as much as possible, but be careful not to tear the skin, especially if you have very small quails. Close the quail up again with a toothpick woven through, as you would pin a hem (if you pin hems – otherwise just use imagination and logic).

Rub each quail with oil and salt, place on a baking tray and roast for 20 minutes or until the flesh is just cooked. If you don't like the idea of slightly pink quail, then add on another 10 minutes, but be careful not to dry out the potentially succulent flesh.

Transfer from the baking tray to plates, pour the piri piri sauce around and about, and serve immediately with vinegary green beans or leaves, plus big finger bowls.

FOR TWO PEOPLE

The quail

2 plump, partially deboned quail (bones in body cavity removed)

Olive oil and salt

Toothpicks for fastening

Macadamia and breadcrumb stuffing

2 slices ciabatta or sourdough, broken into hazelnut-sized bits

½ cup roasted macadamia nuts, chopped up

3 tablespoons olive oil

1 tablespoon chopped coriander leaves

1 tablespoon spring onion

Salt to taste

1 small clove garlic, finely sliced

Piri piri tomato sauce

2 tablespoons fruity, robust olive oil (Portuguese best, but Italian also good)

1 large clove garlic, finely slivered

1 red Thai chilli, finely chopped (or bird's eye for more heat)

½ cup finely chopped tinned tomatoes or one cup skinned, peeled and finely chopped tomato

1 handful Kalamata olives, stoned

½ cup coriander leaves, chopped

Salt to taste – more than you expect

Sugar to balance – around ½ a teaspoon (sauce must not be sweet – add just enough to take the bitter edge off the chilli)

BALINESE **BAKED FISH**

This looks like a mission but it's really just about one shopping trip to procure whatever you don't have (you'll probably find you have half of it already), and then some no-sweat mechanised blending to get everything mashed up. Traditionally, this would be baked in banana leaves, but if you can't get hold of them, reassure yourself that baking paper works perfectly well.

The spice paste makes more than you need, but it's hardly worth making less, and it keeps for ages in the fridge. You can use it later to bake or grill slashed chicken pieces.

Assemble all the paste ingredients.

Preheat the oven to 200 °C.

Grind the peppercorns, nuts and sesame seeds in a spice grinder. Blend this mix with all the remaining paste ingredients in a processor to a smoothish, but not entirely smooth, paste.

Put each fish portion in the middle of a square of baking paper.

Using two heaped teaspoons per portion, spread the paste over both sides of the fish, then fold the papers over loosely to make closed envelopes, fasten with skewer sticks or toothpicks, and bake for 20 minutes.

Serve immediately with steamed long-grain rice and something salady – green, fresh and astringent. The Asian salad on page 54 would be just the thing.

SERVES FOUR

The fish
4 ×150 g extremely fresh fish fillets (white fish, such as sea bass or hake)

4 squares (about 30 × 30 cm) of good-quality baking paper (not the grey butcher paper stuff – it burns)

Spice paste
1½ teaspoons black peppercorns

50 g cashew or macadamia nuts

2 teaspoons sesame seeds

60 g onions, finely chopped

70 g ginger, roughly chopped

1 teaspoon turmeric

3 lemon-grass stalks, roughly chopped

20 g garlic

2 medium-hot chillies, seeds removed

1 heaped tablespoon palm sugar or dark brown sugar

2 teaspoons salt

5 tablespoons vegetable oil

Juice of 1 lime or small lemon

24-HOUR SHOULDER OF PORK

(aka PORK 'DONNIE BRASCO')

Hugh Fearnley-Whittingstall's recipe gets the silly name because, as he describes it, you can 'fugeddaboutit'. And that, in turn, is because it cooks overnight (or for 16 to 24 hours) in the lowest-heat oven imaginable. It is unctuously wonderful in a way that I can't describe. Eat it with steamed rice and an enormous green salad or between slices of soft bread with mustard.

The recipe serves a party of people, and I've left it that way because it seems the right occasion for leaving something in the oven for 24 hours. And a whole pork shoulder is huge – but if you are serving a smaller number, you could ask for a portion of the shoulder, and lower all the quantities in proportion.

I would urge you to seek out properly, humanely, healthily raised pork for this (or any other dish using pork). Intensive pig farming (which accounts for all the default pork out there) is a medievally horrible business. Good butchers, but only a few supermarkets, stock the well-farmed meat.

Preheat the oven to 230 °C. Score the rind of the pork with a Stanley knife in parallel lines about 1 cm apart, almost right through. Mix the garlic and ginger to a paste with the chilli, ground ginger, brown sugar, salt, oil and soy.

Grind the spices in a spice or coffee grinder and mix the ground spice into the paste.

Place the pork skin side up on a rack above a large roasting tray. Rub about half the spice paste into the scored rind. Place the meat in the centre of the hot oven for half an hour. Remove from the oven and, using oven gloves, turn the meat over so the fat is on the bottom. Using a wooden spoon, smear the remaining spice paste on the now top side.

Pour a glass of water into the roasting tin, turn the oven down to 110 °C and put the meat back in. Leave for anything from 16 to 24 hours. After 16 hours check if the pork is ready; if it is, turn off the heat, cover and reheat an hour before serving. If it is not read, keep checking every few hours. Roughly halfway through, turn it skin side up again and baste well with the fat and juices from the roasting tray. Do this again a few hours later.

Thirty minutes before serving, turn the oven back up to 230 °C to crispen the crackling. Watch carefully to make sure it doesn't burn. If it looks like it's blackening in some places too fast, turn the heat down a bit.

To serve, leave the meat to rest for a few minutes, then remove the fatty skin in one piece, or as big pieces as possible, and let everyone take what they want from it. Many large table napkins will be needed. Using a fork or spoon, tear or ease pieces of the meltingly tender meat off the joint. Some fresh chilli in oil goes well on the side, and I like lime wedges too.

Whole shoulder of pork on the bone (about 3 kg)

5 large garlic cloves, peeled and grated

2 pieces fresh ginger, thumb-sized; peeled and grated

2 teaspoons chilli flakes

2 teaspoons ground ginger

1 heaped tablespoon brown sugar

1 tablespoon flake salt (depending on salt brand/type)

1 tablespoon vegetable oil

1 tablespoon soy sauce

Five-spice mix

2 pieces star anise

2 teaspoons fennel seeds (or caraway)

½ cinnamon stick

4 cloves

1 teaspoon black peppercorns

CHILLI, CUMIN & PEANUT LAMB
WITH APPLE-STRIP RELISH

I can't urge you enough to try this flavour bomb from brilliant Adam Liaw, Australian Masterchef winner and author of Two Asian Kitchens, *which you should hastily add to your recipe-book collection. This recipe is a slight adaption of his: I've suggested roasting the lamb rather than deep-frying it, and have added a sharp apple relish on the side in place of his lemon wedges. The lamb is so unctuous that when I eat it I crave the sort of crisp and juicy snap that an apple adds. Eat it with steamed short- or long-grain rice.*

Preheat the oven to 200 °C.

Rub some olive oil over the lamb, grind salt over, and squeeze the lemon on top, then cover loosely with foil and roast for two (shank) to three (leg) hours, or until almost falling off the bone. Don't worry if it's not browned – this will happen next.

Do all the chopping, slicing, etc., while the lamb cooks, and put the apple strips into the lemon juice.

Let the lamb cool, take off the bone in big chunks – tearing rather than cutting – and discard the bigger pieces of fat.

In a heavy-bottomed pan, heat the oil and slow-fry the onion until melty-soft. Remove from the pan.

In the same pan, fry the lamb pieces until dark brown and crusty, then throw in the garlic, fry for a minute, then add the chilli, sugar, peanuts, onions, cumin and, lastly, the soy. Toss together briefly just to heat through. Remove from the heat and mix in the mint and coriander leaves.

Pile onto plates with the lemony apple on the side, lots of steamed long- or short-grain rice and sea-salt flakes.

SERVES FOUR

600 g lamb (small leg or shanks)

Olive oil to rub over lamb

½ teaspoon sea-salt flakes

1 lemon

4 tablespoons peanut or vegetable oil

2 onions, finely slivered

4 garlic cloves, finely slivered

8 or so red chillies (depending on type), seeds removed

1 teaspoon sugar

80 g raw or roasted peanuts

2 tablespoons cumin seeds

2 tablespoons dark soy sauce

2 large handfuls mint leaves

2 large handfuls coriander leaves

Apple relish
4 Granny Smith apples, peeled and julienned (like matchsticks)

Juice of 1 big lemon

LAMPEDUSA PIE

Aka macaroni timbale. Described in luscious detail by Giuseppe Tomasi di Lampedusa in his historical classic, The Leopard, this macaroni and chicken pie, served at a banquet to the last, flailing generation of the Sicilian aristocracy, was something that inhabited our imaginations for years. But for some reason, I only managed to make a facsimile decades later.

When I finally made the timbale, it was wonderful. In truth, of course, nothing can ever really live up to the ever mutable flavours, textures and aromas of a dish only imagined, but I think that even without a whole stash of nostalgia informing your taste buds, this is a very delicious thing indeed.

There are a thousand versions of the timbale. I've chosen this one from the many Italian books that include it, as it seems both the most feasible, and also pretty close to the description in the book (though they would hardly have used instant puff pastry in those days).

Place the chicken with the other chicken ingredients in the cold water, and boil for about an hour and 15 minutes, half covered, until the water has boiled down to one large cup. Remove the chicken and boil the stock further if the stock is not reduced enough. Take the chicken meat off the bones in chunks. Reserve the chicken stock.

Preheat the oven to 180 °C.

Divide the pastry in half. Line the buttered base and sides of a 23 cm pie dish with one half, cover with dried beans, teaspoons, or anything else heatproof that will stop the pastry from puffing up. Bake for 15 minutes or until just turning golden. Remove the weights.

Put the penne on to boil.

Meanwhile, heat the oil in a thick-bottomed pan, then slowly cook the onion down until soft and melty. Remove the onion. Melt the butter in the same pan. Add the flour to the pan and stir through. Add the chicken stock bit by bit, stirring or whisking all the while, until you have a smooth sauce.

Add the cooked onion, wine and spices, and cook for another five minutes or so. Take off the heat. Add the parsley, cheese (and truffle paste if using). Mix in the chicken pieces.

When the pasta is ready, drain well and mix in with the rest of the filling. Add salt and white pepper to taste. Spoon the filling onto the cooked pastry base, level the top, then cover with the other half of the puff pastry. Make patterns as the whim takes you, or leave plain.

(Continued overleaf)

Chicken

1 free-range chicken (or mix of chicken and pigeon)

3 cups water

1 onion

1 bunch parsley

1 teaspoon salt

(see further ingredients for pastry and pie overleaf)

(Lampedusa pie continued)

Bake for 30 minutes, until the pastry is golden-brown.

Leave to rest out of the oven for about 10 minutes to settle, before cutting into thick slices. Eat with something green and simple – vinegared beans, leaves or similar.

SERVES FOUR TO FIVE

Pastry and remaining pie filling

500 g proper butter puff pastry, either home-made or bought (or home-made shortcrust pastry)

1 cup penne (before boiling)

2 tablespoons olive oil

1 onion, very finely chopped

2 heaped tablespoons butter

1 tablespoon flour

½ cup white wine (Chardonnay is good)

½ teaspoon ground cinnamon

¼ teaspoon ground cloves

1 tablespoon finely chopped flat-leaf parsley

2 tablespoons Parmesan

1 teaspoon real truffle paste (optional, really)

Salt and white pepper to taste

OLD CHINATOWN

What a wonderful place Johannesburg's first Chinatown was. Spanning the last few blocks of Commissioner Street and ending just across the road from what I still think of as John Vorster Square, it was one of the city's greatest eating strips. Going to feast on yum cha at the Golden Palace on a Sunday was glorious. It was a huge, even grand, eatery filled with very loud diners (most of them Chinese, but many others not), waitresses pushing around trolleys stacked high with bamboo steamers filled with dumplings, and always a lot of drinking and smoking going on. Tables were filled with groups of 10 or more. Whether or not the sun was over the yardarm was of no relevance – many were breakfasting with whiskys and G & Ts to accompany. It closed down a long time ago, somewhere in the mid-1990s, I think.

There were so many other wonderful places, among them the corner deli one block down from the Golden Palace, which made huge steel-and-bamboo baskets of takeaway bao (steamed buns), fish-stuffed green peppers and fried chicken on Sundays. It was so full of people queueing for the hot stuff you could hardly move. That deli is long gone. In about 1992, I think, it turned into a laundry for a while, and is now boarded up.

The last tiny restaurant on the strip, or cornering the strip, was legendary. The customers at Chon Hing were of an exotic and impressive bent, it seemed to me in my late teens and twenties. There were always press photographers and lawyers with famous political clients, plus anyone who could flick a brush at a canvas. The square and efficient owner, Yvonne, ran hither and thither with the platters while her two children and husband sat and watched TV in the narrow passageway between the kitchen and the tables. Yvonne had to pass in front of them about a million times a shift, often pushing their legs to the side as she passed. Never once, in decades, did they offer to help with one dish, one serviette, one fallen grain of rice. I even felt a bit mean eating there – another table, another batch of plates to carry was all I could think. To add to her gruelling routine, the place had half the tables in the basement, reached via killer-pitched stairs. Yvonne may have looked square, but under that workwear she must surely have had damn fine legs. It's closed now, of course. I so hope Yvonne is sitting in front of an even bigger TV having a rest, and being brought something dumplingy on a tray by her now grown children. Probably not.

One of the best things from that street was anything they did with greens at Yung Chen Noodle Den, just around the corner. This micro-eatery, my favourite of all, was the most recent to fall. Last time I drove there craving a bowl of greens and a seaweed salad, I was met by a new sign on the door which told me 'wors and pap R15'. Now, I like wors and pap too, but sometimes living in a city that's so rabidly in flux can be trying – especially when you have a growling bok choy craving to satisfy.

LAMPEDUSA PIE

BRIGHT-GREEN **BOK CHOY**

The Cantonese way of cooking these vegetables at theYung Chen Noodle Den leaves them brilliantly green, shiny and succulent, and retaining all the flavour they were born with. Very high, very fast cooking, and sometimes blanching before, does the trick, whether semi-braised in a wok or thrown into the rolling boil of a broth near the end. You can also cook young green beans, Swiss chard and small leeks this way.

I describe here the wok method, for which you can of course use a really big pan, but I think every kitchen is happier with at least one proper steel wok. Don't skimp on the oil, no matter how tempted you are. If you're not vegetarian, you can happily throw in some chicken stock or chicken fat at the end, as they often do in the restaurants. It adds incredible flavour.

Boil the kettle. Place the greens in a large bowl, and pour boiling water over them to cover well. After 10 seconds or so, drain and cover the greens with cold water. Drain again. (Less annoying than it sounds.)

Toss the greens with the vegetable oil, and throw into a very hot wok. Add the garlic and/or ginger after about half a minute. Don't crowd the vessel, as the heat will drop too much. Add the salt, toss about for half a minute more or until just wilted, taste and adjust the salt amount if you need to. Add a shake of sesame oil, and serve. Eat as a side dish or just with lots or steaming rice and fresh chilli.

SERVES TWO

2 big handfuls bok choy, gai larn (most delicious) or other greens, cut through lengthwise for quicker cooking

2 tablespoons vegetable oil

1 heaped tablespoon slivered ginger and/or 2 teaspoons slivered garlic (The Cantonese go with only one or the other at a time in this dish. I, in a no doubt cretinous move, include them both.)

Salt to taste (or, as is protocol in many restaurants, some MSG – no joke)

Shake of sesame oil

BEST-EVER **CINNAMON-FUDGE SAUCE**

Here is a sauce that turns decent people savage. Whether or not that is a recommendation will depend on your entertaining style. If you burn the sugar to a really dark brown, which takes a little more nerve than whipping it off the heat when just turning amber, this sauce has a wonderful smoky depth, rather than just being sweet. The cinnamon also adds a layer of flavour that stops it from being flatly saccharine.

It's very simple to make and light years away from any commercial fudge product out there. I like it best hot, in a bowl into which you've sliced bananas or nectarines alongside good vanilla ice cream (add only the amount of ice cream that you need per bite, because it's the still-hot sauce mixing with ice cream in your mouth that's so blissful).

Melt the sugar and butter slowly until the sugar is mushy and dissolving.

Keep on a moderate heat, stirring now and then, until the sugar caramelises, and starts to go really dark brown. Stir constantly while this is happening, and when it looks as if going any darker will result in burnt (sort of crème caramel base stage), chuck in the cream.

It will bubble and go mad, and form crystal lumps; just ignore them and keep on a low heat to let all the lumps dissolve, stirring every now and then. It might take up to 20 minutes to get smooth again. Add the cinnamon now if in stick form.

If it is taking too long and the sauce is getting too thick, add more cream, or even water, to get back to almost the same volume you had in the beginning. (Drop a blob into cold water to test; it should be like thick honey when room temperature, liquid when hot.)

Remove the cinnamon stick and stir in the salt. Strain out any lumps with which you've lost patience. Add the cinnamon if in ground form.

This sauce keeps bottled in the fridge for months, or at room temperature for about a week.

MAKES ABOUT ONE CUP OF SAUCE (YOU BE THE JUDGE OF HOW MANY THIS MIGHT SERVE)

1 cup light brown sugar

2 tablespoons butter

1 cup single cream

2 cinnamon sticks or ½ teaspoon ground cinnamon (if using cinnamon sticks, add with the cream; if ground, add right at the end)

Pinch of salt (I like it really salty, but you can also just serve flake salt next to it, which is almost painfully good)

LAMPEDUSA PIE

BEER CAKE

I don't particularly like beer as a straight-up drink, but I crave it in cooking. My German granny came to stay with us over a long, really hot summer when I was very little, and she made us hot, milky beer soup (certainly not your regular Highveld heatwave snack). I remember sitting on the kitchen counter next to a soup pot, which in my memory held enough soup to feed 30 people, being fed small cupfuls, and just loving it. Everyone else ran away from the stuff but I found the sweet-sour oddness of the thing totally addictive.

I'm not about to give you a recipe for said soup – I doubt there'd be many takers. But the recipe I fell upon for beer cake recently hits almost the same yeasty-malty, sweet-sour spot, and is an easier ride. It's now one of my all-time favourite cakes. This is a heavy cake though, something like a pound cake, and I'm emphasising this because it's the sort of cake that we're not used to any more... so be warned if you think that might not be your thing. It's at its best still warm from the oven, with some pouring cream.

Preheat the oven to 180 °C.

Line a standard (24 cm) round cake tin (or equivalent volume square tin) with baking paper.

For the topping, mix the flour, cinnamon, sugar and butter, till you have the texture of rough sand.

For the base, beat the butter with the sugar until pale and creamy. Add the eggs and sifted flour alternately. Fold in the flour, raisins and beer. Pour the mixture into the prepared tin, and sprinkle the topping evenly over the top.

Bake for 1½ hours or just until a skewer comes out clean. At the halfway mark, turn the oven down to 160 °C.

Let the cake cool slightly before attacking. Serve with lots of cream, ice cream or custard on the side. Or, now that I think about it, stewed, spiced apples might be nicest of all.

Topping

250 ml cake flour

3 ml ground cinnamon

250 ml light brown sugar

125 ml butter

Base

125 ml + 1 heaped tablespoon butter

500 ml sugar

3 eggs

560 g self-raising flour

250 ml raisins

500 ml beer (lager style or similar)

DATE, TAMARIND & WALNUT CAKE

Inspired by a recipe from the great baker Dan Lepard, this is a very grown-up cake, which – if my tasting sample of 10 children is anything to go by – is widely disliked by anyone under 12. It's the very things that the under-12s can't abide that give it the allure missing from most flatly sweet cakes. The weird sourness of tamarind against the sticky sweetness of the dates and the warmth of the walnuts and spice combine to make this one of the most satisfying cakes you will ever bite into.

On day one, it's moist and almost pudding-like, and wants to be eaten with some cream or custard. Then, strangely, on days two, three and four, it turns into something close to date loaf or gingerbread, and cries out to be eaten topped with slabs of cold butter. In fact, the nature of the cake on these later days makes me think that you should cook it in a large loaf tin or a square cake tin, and not, as I did, in a round tin, which really seems a bit at odds with the cake's character.

Heat the oven to 180 °C.

Place the dates in a large bowl, pour the water over them and leave to soak.

Put a large heatproof bowl on your kitchen scales, set the scales back to zero and measure in the butter (chopped up), syrup (poured straight from the tin or it's such a mess) and tamarind.

Place the bowl in the warming-up oven and leave till the butter is melted, but not bubbling and boiling. Remove from the oven and stir to combine.

Add the sugar and eggs, mixing in thoroughly.

Next add the flour and spices, then the nuts and finally the dates with their soaking water. Mix everything together well.

Pour into a lined 24 cm spring-form cake tin or a square tin of similar size, and cook for about 50 minutes or just until a skewer or knife comes out clean.

Try to avoid cutting the cake until it's cooled down for at least 10 minutes, or it will break up.

250 g pitted dates (to avoid losing teeth, check that each one is properly pitted)

280 ml boiling water

250 g butter

50 g golden syrup

50 g deseeded tamarind paste (you can get this from most Asian and Indian superettes)

100 g dark/treacle sugar

2 eggs

275 g self-raising flour

2 teaspoons cinnamon

½ teaspoon ground cloves

½ teaspoon nutmeg

250 g chopped walnuts or pecan nuts

ACKNOWLEDGEMENTS

This book might have my name on the cover, but of course almost all the recipes inside are only 'my' recipes in the most oblique and partial way. Unless there is a long-lost cookbook written by Adam and Eve (messes of pottage galore, I imagine), this is the case for any cookbook ever written. All recipe compilations are far more about influence and limitation and far less about inspiration and originality than they appear. So to all the people I haven't named but who are part of this unseen web, both dead and alive, I owe thanks.

Bigger thanks go to the people closer to me. To my ever-supportive parents, who took my brother and me to eat so many great meals in so many great places all through our ridiculously lucky childhoods.

To Nick, the most wonderful husband imaginable. He has only two flaws: he doesn't feel very passionate about dim sum, and he has little time for stinky cheese. Only two, imagine that.

To my lovely children, Jim, Holly and Thomas, who are always brutally, helpfully honest about my cooking forays and are my favourite people in the world to cook for.

To Leah Tsonye, incredible cook, great friend, and an inspiration to me.

To Terry Morris from Pan Macmillan and Louise Grantham from Bookstorm, who have been the most amazing publishers anyone on earth could ever hope for. I fell with my bum in the butter (home-made) with both of you. To brilliant photographer Theana Breugem, who has made this book beautiful, and managed to do so while dodging dogs chasing cats, sticky children's fingers and woks on fire, often while balancing on a ladder. To René de Wet, who designed this book so perfectly and with such good humour in the face of constant changes and time pressure.

Thank you.

INDEX

Text © Andrea Burgener
Photographs © Theana Breugem

All rights reserved. No part of this book may be reproduced or transmitted in any form or by any means, electronic or mechanical, including photocopying, recording or any information storage or retrieval system, without permission from the copyright holder.

ISBN: 978-1-920434-45-8

First edition, first impression 2013

Published jointly by Bookstorm (Pty) Ltd, PO Box 4532, Northcliff 2115, Johannesburg, South Africa, www.bookstorm.co.za and Pan Macmillan South Africa, Private Bag X19, Northlands 2116, Johannesburg, South Africa, www.panmacmillan.co.za

Distributed by Pan Macmillan
via Booksite Afrika

Edited by Mark Ronan
Proofread by John Henderson
Photography by Theana Breugem
Cover and design by René de Wet
Printed by Ultra Litho (Pty) Ltd, Johannesburg